Reader-Friendly Reports

Reader-Friendly Reports

A No-Nonsense Guide to

EFFECTIVE WRITING

for MBAs, Consultants, and Other Professionals

CARTER A. DANIEL

New York Chicago San Francisco Lisbon London Madrid Mexico City
Milan New Delhi San Juan Seoul Singapore Sydney Toronto

1 2 3 4 5 6 7 8 9 10 QFR/QFR 1 9 8 7 6 5 4 3 2 1

ISBN   978-0-07-178285-2
MHID   0-07-178285-0

e-ISBN   978-0-07-178286-9
e-MHID 0-07-178286-9

McGraw-Hill books are available at special quantity discounts to use as
premiums and sales promotions or for use in corporate training programs.
To contact a representative, please e-mail us at bulksales@mcgraw-hill.com.

This book is printed on acid-free paper.

If we have to choose between candidates who can write well and candidates who know accounting well, we choose the ones who can write. We can teach accounting principles in a few weeks, but bad writing creates such a drag on performance we just prefer not to get involved.

—the Senior Vice President of a major bank in New York

Never, for even a moment, let out of your sight the single purpose of business writing: to persuade your reader, as efficiently as possible, of the validity of your thesis.

We are aiming here at two things: instant accessibility and absolute unmisunderstandability.

Keep in mind Daniel's First Law:
Organize around conclusions.
And Daniel's Second Law:
Tell people what you're going to say before you say it.

Contents

III. Research Techniques 117

VI. The Appearance of the Finished Document 185

Appendix: Checklists 193

Part I

PLANNING A READER-FRIENDLY REPORT

RIGHT AND WRONG, BOSS AND BOOK

For some reason, questions of writing style and correctness bring out people's most mule-headed private opinions. A boss who doesn't know anything about calculus or linear programming would never think of overruling a subordinate on one of those subjects. But just let that same subordinate do something contrary to what the boss's ignorant sixth-grade teacher said—some asinine rule about not ending a sentence with a preposition or not starting one with *and* or *because*—and the boss will pounce with fangs bared.

Such a situation is much more political than it is intellectual, and the moral to be drawn from it is that if somebody is paying your salary, you should write the way that person wants. Writing is far less often "right" or "wrong" than it is "appropriate" or "inappropriate." Obviously, if you write in a way that irritates your boss, you're writing inappropriately.

This manual sets forth some reasonable suggestions about decent business writing—suggestions you might want to follow if you haven't been given any specific rules to govern the particular task you're doing. Everything that is said here, however, should be considered subject to being overruled by any special requirements you have been given for a particular assignment.

Just to make sure it's clear, let's say it one more time, a different way: For the love of mud, whatever you do, don't go wave this book in your boss's face and shout, "See? You're wrong!" When your boss tells you one thing and the book tells you something different, do what your boss says.

WHAT BUSINESS WRITING ISN'T AND IS

Business writing isn't a different language with a separate set of words and phrases. *In receipt of, as per your request, beg to acknowledge,* and *please be advised* are relics of the past. They aren't used anymore, or shouldn't be anyway.

Business writing also isn't dull and stereotyped. Bad writing is dull; good writing is interesting. These statements are true for all writing, business or any other kind. If you are interested in a subject but find the report dull, something's wrong with the way the report is written.

Business writing is just like any other writing except more efficient. Whereas some kinds of writing aim at being dreamy, witty, entertaining, spooky, outrageous, shocking, or sexy, when you're doing the kind of writing being described here you have only one aim: to persuade your reader, as efficiently as possible, of the validity of your thesis.

Think for a minute about who your audience is, and you'll understand the reason for insisting on efficiency. Businesspeople are intelligent, suspicious, and busy. So when you write for them you have to be factual, persuasive, and efficient: factual because they are too intelligent to be fooled by vagueness and bluffing; persuasive because you have to overcome the suspicion that always accompanies money matters; and efficient because you'll lose your reader if you waste time.

A few pages from now (page 9, to be exact) you will encounter a description of the thesis-and-subheaded-structured-segments organization, the standard pattern for organizing business reports. Even before you get there, however, you might do well to think for a moment about the whole reason for organizing a business report differently from the way you organize a magazine article, a novel, or an advertisement. Try this explanation:

The people who assigned you the report did so because they didn't have time to do the work themselves. They asked you the questions, and now they want the answers. The answers are, therefore, the most important things in your report, and you must organize your whole report around those answers and wave them in your readers' faces. State the answers at the beginning; elaborate on them one by one in the rest of the report; include only things that pertain to these answers; and be sure that the pertinence is always clear. Reread this paragraph.

Or, to be still more specific, don't say anything that isn't part of the answer to the question you were asked. Don't restate the problem, or announce that you have finished researching it, or summarize the background, or spend time defining terms, or tell about how you made your calculations or classified your evidence. Just answer the bleeding question, starting at the very very beginning. You may reread this paragraph too.

To put it still another way, don't say something unless you're making some point by saying it. If, for instance, there's nothing in the company's history that has any relevance to the problem, then in the name of good sense don't go into the company's history. On the other hand, if the company's problems are partly traceable to the fact that it has always been family owned, then by all means do tell the history—making sure, every moment, that the point of your telling it is clear.

Help your reader every way you can. Be certain that the point of each paragraph is clear. After you've finished writing, go back and check each one of them to see if you can state its point in a quick phrase and to see if each of these phrases fits in with the thesis. Even if the report is short, use subheadings not merely (1) to demarcate the segments but more importantly (2) to let the readers know what they're getting ready to read. And remember to include in your report only what your first paragraph promised. Never, for even a moment, let out of your sight the purpose of a business report: to convince your reader, as efficiently as possible, of the validity of your thesis. (More, as noted before, starting on page 9.)

Practice: What to Include in a Report

Petunia Newcomer, writing her first report, asks you, an experienced employee, "Are we supposed to include some background on the company when we write these reports?" Sonny Arrivato, also writing his first, says "How long is the report supposed to be?" Answer them both. (Begin your answer, "Listen, blockheads.")

UNDERSTANDING THE ASSIGNMENT

Before starting to answer the question, you've got to know what the question is. A sizable portion of business writing troubles can be traced to a failure to identify the assignment correctly. For example, although asked what to do about a problem, an incompetent report writer might waste the entire report telling instead how the problem occurred, which isn't the same thing at all. As a result, the reader has to suffer through the whole tedious report without ever finding out the answer to the question. Likewise if the boss asks a supervisor to recommend for or against promotion of an employee, but the supervisor instead spends the whole report recounting the employee's work history and never gets around to the yes-or-no recommendation, the boss will be furious—and should be, too, because it's a bad report.

The importance of this point can't be overstated: if you don't get the assignment right, if you don't answer the right question, then no amount of "good writing" or "extensive research" or "penetrating analysis" can salvage your report. You're fired.

Try writing out the specific question that you think your report is supposed to answer. That way, if you don't have a clear enough picture of the assignment, you'll quickly sense there's a problem. Be especially wary when your instructions contain words like "look into" or "analyze" or "see what you can find out about," because you need to know something more specific than just that to do a good job.

ASSESSING THE AUDIENCE

Likewise, before you start writing your report, be sure you know who you're writing to. Writing is, as page 3 said, less often "right" or "wrong" than it is "appropriate" or "inappropriate," and what's appropriate for one reader can be wildly off-center for another. For instance, what's exactly suited for a general audience of outsiders is unsuited (and boring) for insiders who know the technical language. Likewise, somebody who has asked you a question will simply be irritated if you spend half your report repeating the question; but on the other hand somebody who doesn't even know what the question was will be lost if you don't repeat it.

In assessing your audience you should determine the answers to two questions: (1) How much can you omit because the reader already knows it? and (2) How much technical knowledge does the reader have? Once you have the answers, follow these two rules: omit as much as possible, and be as technical as possible. Any other way of writing is inefficient and runs the risk of boring—and insulting—your readers.

Of course you need to think of more than just those two things. You have to figure out what your readers are looking for—that is, what they are going to be expecting when they pick up your report. If you try to be funny when they are being serious, or if you try to be leisurely when they're in a hurry, you will have magisterially screwed up. Think very carefully about the whole question. Put yourself in the position of the person your message is intended for, and try to imagine how you would react if you received a report like the one you have just written. Don't underestimate the importance of this part of the job.

DETERMINING THE CONTROLLING PURPOSE

The single most important element in achieving understandability, efficiency, clarity, and persuasiveness is *control*. Every sentence, every paragraph, and especially the report as a whole must be firmly controlled by a governing purpose.

From the very first, the reader must be able to see what the purpose of the report is. Then, in each paragraph, it must be absolutely clear to the reader what point is being made there. Even each individual sentence must relate in some clearly perceptible way to the ones preceding it. In this way the reader will never have to wonder, "Why am I being told all this? When will it get to the point?"

It should come as no shock, therefore, that formulating the purpose is the most important chore facing the writer. Most business writing problems—around 95 percent probably—can be traced to writers' lack of clarity about what they want to say. Bad writers always complain, "I know what I want to say, but when I sit down to write I can't say it." Baaaaaaloney. The truth is that they just *think* they know what they want to say: it's only when they start to write that they find they haven't really got it figured out at all. If they really knew what they wanted to say, right down to the little details, then saying it would be a snap.

Thus writing serves an additional purpose: besides communicating ideas to others, it is a way for writers to make sure their ideas are clear to themselves.

Corny Analogy. In an ordinary metal bar, the disarranged atoms point randomly in every direction. But when a strong magnetic field is brought to act on the bar, the atoms come into alignment so that they all point to the same end. As a result, the bar then picks up a magnetic force of its own.

A report in which the parts are disarranged and not clearly pointing in the same direction is lifeless and ineffectual. But when a strong controlling purpose aligns the parts of the report so that they all point to the same end, the whole report acquires a persuasive force of its own.

ORGANIZING A REPORT

Set forth in the next dozen pages of this manual is the *thesis-and-subheaded-structured-segments organization pattern*, the standard and most unmisunderstandable organization for use in business reports. What it does is to have you set out the parts of your argument in a systematic way and to let your reader know how you've done it so it will be easy to follow.

In three sentences, the "thesis-and-subheaded-structured-segments" pattern looks like this:

- The first paragraph states the thesis in such a way that the reader can tell (1) *what* the rest of the report will say and (2) *in what order* the material will be presented.
- Then the rest of the report goes on to follow exactly the order set up in the first paragraph, with segments clearly and visibly demarcated with thesis-like subheadings, so that the reader can tell where one part stops and the next part starts and can tell in advance what point each upcoming section is going to make.
- And the segments themselves are also carefully structured, so that they state the point, explain how it is to be presented, give the supporting details, and then summarize it.

This organizational pattern is the most basic characteristic of business report writing. You must use it. It not only helps the reader but clarifies and simplifies things for the writer too. Yet some people—all the way up through the almost-boardroom in business and the almost-Ph.D. in school—never do learn how, and they remain "almosts" all their lives as a result.

First, you need to be sure you recognize the difference between a thesis and a topic; then you need to know how to state the thesis in the first paragraph; next you need to know what the subheadings look like; and finally you need to understand how to structure a paragraph.

Here goes.

Recognizing the Difference between a Topic and a Thesis

The topic is what you're writing about; the thesis is what you say about your topic. The topic is the question you've been asked to find an answer to; the thesis is the answer you find. The topic is generally assigned to you by your boss; the thesis is what you conclude after you've done all the research.

"The advisability of trying to acquire full or part ownership of the Schlerg Company" is a topic. "The Schlerg Company is not a suitable target for acquisition" is a thesis. See the difference?

Notice how much time and work elapsed between those two sentences. The topic is the question, and the thesis is its answer. Between the question and the answer lie all the hours (or weeks, or months) of research and study.

Thus another word for thesis is answer. Another is point. Another is conclusion. Another is findings. Another is object. Another is purpose.

Now try your hand at recognizing a topic and a thesis.

Practice: Topic or Thesis?

Tell whether each of the following is a topic or a thesis.

1. The Schlerg Company

   _____

2. The Schlerg Company's sales

   _____

3. The decline in the Schlerg Company's sales

   _____

4. The reasons for the decline in the Schlerg Company's sales

   _____

5. Poor management practices within and aggressive competition without have caused the decline in the Schlerg Company's sales.

   _____

6. Poor management practices and aggressive competition

   _____

7. Poor management practices

   _____

8. Management

   _____

9. The decreased importance of insurance, and increased importance of retailing, in the Schlerg Company's future

   _____

10. At the Schlerg Company, insurance is decreasing in importance, and retailing is increasing.

    _____

11. The Empire State Building in New York is one of the tallest buildings in the world.

    _____

Answers are given on the next page.

Stating the Thesis in the First Paragraph

Get straight to the point. In the first few lines, you must tell both *what* you have found out in your research and *in what order* you are going to present the explanation of your findings. "I recommend that we do not consider Mr. Nerf for the controller's position, because of his undistinguished past performance, his questionable integrity, and his abrasive personality"—that's a good thesis sentence. The first part tells *what* (I don't recommend him), and the second part tells *what order* (my three reasons).

Writers often—very often—screw up right at this point. It is therefore most important that you learn now exactly what is and what isn't acceptable as a thesis statement and how to go about formulating a good one.

Suppose, for example, you have been asked to look into the Schlerg Company as a possible acquisition by your company. After long hours of research, you have come up with the following 11 pieces of information:

Schlerg's sales have declined during all but one of the past eight years.

The company's debt/equity ratio is 8:1.

Five strikes have occurred in the last six years.

Company officers have denied persistent rumors that a pension fund scandal exists.

The government has awarded back pay to three of seven women who claimed discrimination.

Schlerg's stock is mentioned in *Forbes* as overpriced.

Environmental organizations have reportedly singled out Schlerg for boycott because of water pollution.

The Secretary of Labor alluded sarcastically to Schlerg during a recent address to the AFL-CIO.

The owners have charged workers with deliberately sabotaging machinery.

The state health department will investigate charges of excess radiation at two of Schlerg's plants.

Several minority-rights groups include Schlerg on their recommended boycott list.

Clearly the evidence shows that the company is bad news; you already know what your recommendation will be. The only decision you face is how to present the evidence so persuasively that your reader will agree with your point.

One possible way—the wrongest one—is simply to give the evidence as it happened to turn up in this list. Thus your report would blurt out that "Schlerg-is-an-undesirable-acquisition-because-of-declining-sales-poor-debt-equity-ratio-strikes-scandal-rumors-sex-discrimination-overpriced-stock-reported-environmen-talists-boycott-Labor-Secretary-slur-alleged-sabotage-alleged-health-hazard-and-possible-minority-boycott." Of course that approach is the worst you could use, because it has little persuasive force and no memorability at all; in fact nobody (including you, right?) can remember half the points it made, and nobody can even come close to remembering the order they're in.

So instead, try grouping the points by subject. You will quickly see that a few major categories stand out:

Declining sales	Financial
High debt-equity ratio	Financial
Strikes	Labor relations
Scandal rumors	Public relations
Sex discrimination cases	Labor relations
Overpriced stock	Financial
Environmentalist boycott	Public relations
Labor Secretary slur	Public relations
Sabotage charge	Labor relations
Health hazard charge	Public relations
Minority boycott	Public relations

Now you can tell your reader that Schlerg has three undesirable qualities—poor finances, poor labor relations, and poor public relations—and any reader (including you, right?) can easily remember all three points.

All that's left to do now is to put it all together in a thesis paragraph. Look how easy it is:

> The Schlerg Company is not a desirable acquisition for us because of problems
> it has been experiencing in finances, labor relations, and public relations.

Anybody reading this one opening sentence knows immediately not just *what* the point is but *in what order* the reasons will be presented. And it's all easy to remember, too.

Practice: Avoiding Common Errors in Thesis Paragraphs

Since it's so important, pause here for a while to see if you can detect what's wrong with each of the following thesis paragraphs. All are bad, and all the errors are common ones.

1. As you requested, I have spent some time investigating the feasibility of acquiring the Schlerg Company. I have now completed the research and wish to present my findings to you in the following report.

2. A boycott by minority groups and another one by environmentalists, along with a high debt-equity ratio and five strikes in six years, not to mention possible health hazards and a charge of sabotage, besides declining sales, rumors of a scandal, a slur by the Labor Secretary, sex discrimination, and overpriced stock, make Schlerg a poor choice.

3. The Schlerg Company has experienced five strikes in the last six years. From the evidence I have been able to gather, it appears that some of them were justified and some not.

4. Having completed my research on Schlerg, I am now presenting my report. After first stating my recommendations, I will go on to present my reasons.

5. The possibility of acquiring Schlerg raises many interesting questions, including some in finance, labor relations, and public relations.

6. The following report analyzes the financial situation, employee relations, and public image of the Schlerg Company. Following these analyses, the recommendation will be made.

7. The Schlerg Company, founded in 1953 and run exclusively by members of the Schlerg family ever since, is best known for its line of household products. It has three plants, in New Jersey, Kansas, and Oregon, in order to permit quick distribution. Corporate headquarters is in East Orange, New Jersey.

8. Because of your interest in acquiring attractive companies, you have asked me to look into the possibility and desirability of our buying all or part of the Schlerg Company.

9. I do not recommend that we consider acquiring the Schlerg Company, for three reasons.

10. I recommend against acquiring the Schlerg Company for three reasons. The first is financial, under which heading I will discuss the declining sales, the poor debt-equity ratio, and the overpriced stock. Second is the labor strife, which has been evident in strikes, sex discrimination suits, and possible sabotage. The third reason is the poor public relations, with two boycotts, rumors of a scandal, a slur by the Secretary of Labor, and a State Health Department investigation.

Now, just to clean the air, take a look at three good ones:

> The Schlerg Company is not a desirable acquisition for us because of problems it has been experiencing in finances, labor relations, and public relations.

Or slightly expanded:

> The Schlerg Company is not a desirable acquisition because of problems it has been experiencing in finances, labor relations, and public relations. Therefore I strongly urge that we forget all about any connection with Schlerg and instead turn our attention elsewhere.

Or another variation:

> The Schlerg Company has been experiencing some serious problems in finance, labor relations, and public relations. For these reasons it is clearly an undesirable target for takeover, and I therefore think we should cease any further consideration of it and instead should look elsewhere for acquisitions.

What-and-what-order thesis paragraphs thus allow plenty of room for individuality and experimentation; they don't all have to be exactly alike.

Remember where you are in all this now? You have learned (a) how to distinguish between a topic and a thesis and (b) how to construct a what-and-what-order thesis paragraph. All that's left now is to learn (c) how to use subheadings to demarcate and introduce the subsequent segments and then (d) how to structure the segments effectively. (Part d—the structure of segments—will be the subject of Part II.)

Constructing Subheaded Segments

Since you have just constructed a thesis paragraph that tells what order your report will take, all you have to do now is to follow that announced order. Suppose, to go back to the earlier example, your thesis paragraph said "I recommend that we do not consider Mr. Nerf for the controller's position because of his mediocre past performance, his questionable integrity, and his abrasive personality." Obviously, the rest of your report will fall into three parts, dealing with performance, integrity, and personality. What you have to do is to demarcate and introduce those three parts so that the reader (1) will clearly see where one part stops and the next starts and (2) will be told in advance exactly what each new point is going to say before it actually gets presented.

Notice the word "point" here. It was point (= *thesis*, = *conclusion*, = *findings*, = *purpose*), not *topic*. It is not, repeat NOT, enough merely to label Part 1 "Performance," Part 2 "Integrity," and Part 3 "Personality." The job of a subheading is not just to demarcate but to introduce too. You must head the segments in such a way that your reader knows not only the name of the topic that the segment will discuss but what point is going to be made *about* the topic. In the example just mentioned, all you have to do is add a descriptive word to each of the topics: instead of "Performance," "Integrity," and "Personality," say "Mediocre Performance," "Questionable Integrity," and "Abrasive Personality." That way, the reader is reminded not just of what the topics are but of what you're going to say about them.

The demarcation can take either of two formats—keywords or separate (and maybe numbered) subheadings, as shown in the illustrations on page 18. Both are easy to read and universally acceptable, the only distinction being that keywords are best used when you have just a few uncomplicated points. When the organization is even slightly complex, subheadings are better because they have more versatility and visibility.

Either way, remember: (1) you **must have a subheading**, and (2) the subheading **must be thesis-like, must be a mini-thesis, must point a direction, must state a subconclusion**. Just stating the subject, like "performance" or "integrity" or "personality," isn't ever enough. Remind the reader what it is that you are going to say in the upcoming segment about performance and integrity and personality.

Keep in mind, whether you use keywords or subheadings on a separate line, that the purpose of having such devices is threefold: (1) to enable your readers to jump ahead to any section, in a sort of random-access system; (2) to indicate unmistakably where one section stops and the next starts; and (3) to jog your readers' memories at each new section, telling them in advance what the section is going to say.

In business reports you must use one or the other of these methods—keywords or subheadings—since you simply cannot leave these things to chance. Don't let your readers have even the slightest excuse to say they couldn't follow what you were saying.

Okay—here are the illustrations. The one on the left uses subheadings on a separate line; the one on the right uses keywords. Both are equally acceptable.

To: Mr. Emerson
From: Egbert Egbert
Subject: Mr. Nerf
Date: 3/5/20—

I recommend that we do not consider Mr. Nerf for the Controller's position because of his mediocre past performance, his questionable integrity, and his abrasive personality.

Past Performance Not Good

Over the past five years, Mr. Nerf has rarely met his goals and has never received a commendation from his supervisors. He failed to develop the new system for tracking overdue accounts as he was assigned. He barely increased collections from overdue accounts last

To: Mr. Emerson
From: Egbert Egbert
Subject: Mr. Nerf
Date: 3/5/20—

I recommend that we do not consider Mr. Nerf for the Controller's position because of his mediocre past performance, his questionable integrity, and his abrasive personality.

Poor Performance. Over the past five years, Mr. Nerf has rarely met his goals and has never received a commendation from his supervisors. He failed to develop the new system for tracking overdue accounts as he was assigned. He barely increased collections from overdue accounts last

AFTERWORD

Two final thoughts about planning and organizing.

The great majority of problems with business reports come from defective thinking and planning rather than defective writing. Thus the section you have just finished reading—"Planning a Reader-Friendly Report"—is the most important part of this book. Once the ideas are in place, nearly everything else in a report follows easily.

Second, remember especially that the first paragraph is the make- or break-all. It sets the tone, establishes the organization, and gives your readers confidence in you—or turns them off. Your readers can walk away anytime they want, and the first paragraph is where they decide whether or not they want to stay. To say it again, and probably not for the last time either: the opening paragraph of a business report must state the thesis in such a way that the reader can tell (1) *what* the rest of the report will say and (2) *in what order* the material will be presented. What and what order—these must be clear by the end of the first paragraph.

PART II

WRITING A READER-FRIENDLY REPORT

UNDERSTANDABILITY

The reason for writing well rather than badly is, of course, to make your reader's job easier. Anything that makes your point easier to understand is good; anything that makes it less easy is bad. Understandability—the ease with which your point can be understood—is the only criterion for determining what is good writing. Reading is, after all, hard enough even when the writing is good; bad writing simply creates unnecessary obstacles that make understanding even harder.

The five most common impediments to understandability are these:

Failure to be neat
Failure to write grammatically
Failure to write appropriately and effectively
Failure to organize
Failure to make the organizational plan clear

Avoid all five of these and you'll be the best writer in the company.

Since impediments 4 and 5—the organization ones—have already been dealt with in Part I, the present section will treat only (1) failure to be neat, (2) failure to write grammatically, and (3) failure to write appropriately and effectively.

Failure to Be Neat

In an age when sloppiness has become almost a virtue, when indifference to appearance is seen as a mark of importance and dash, nobody thinks messiness and unattractiveness are important obstacles. But they are, for two specific reasons.

The first is that if you don't make people want to read your work and don't also make it easy for them to do so, they won't. All those years in school—where teachers got paid to read writing whether or not they wanted to—have spoiled us and made us forget that once we get out of school, nobody ever again has to read anything we write.

And for sure, anybody who doesn't have to, anybody who has a choice, will refuse to read a report printed with a faded gray printer cartridge, or printed on transparent tissue paper, or single-spaced, or jammed against the left and right and top and bottom edges without any margins. As was just said, reading is tough at best, so the least a writer can do is to remove all the physical obstacles—to make it look good so that people (maybe even teachers) will want to read it.

Second, if the appearance of a report is slovenly, readers will think the content is too. Experiments have repeatedly demonstrated that two versions of the same piece of writing, one attractive and one sloppy, elicit different responses from their readers. Readers think, quite understandably, that a report that looks like garbage, is garbage—that a writer who doesn't bother about appearance didn't bother about the content either. Just remember how turned off you are by books that have blindingly dark typefaces or squintingly tiny print, or by posters that instead of looking professional look like something the third grade would have discarded. Appearance does matter.

To the scoffer who snorts, "Did it ever occur to you there might be some good ideas in the report? Aren't you even concerned about that? So all you worry about is looks already?," the answer resounds like this: That's the whole point, Oatmeal-brain. If the paper is wrongheaded and stupid, then who cares if it doesn't get read? The problem comes up only when somebody does go to great pains to write a profound, original, important report and then blows it all by failing to take those last few minutes to see that the report looks as good as it is.

Put it another way: What difference does it make how good the ideas are if nobody is going to read it?

Details on what constitutes neatness are given in Part VI, "The Appearance of the Finished Document." For right now, pay attention to at least these basic rules:

- Double-space all typed work, except letters.
- Leave huge margins, including at the top and bottom.
- Write on one side only.

- Number your pages.
- In general, be sure your work is **instantly legible**, so that your reader has to devote no effort at all to deciphering it. A document should contain no surface static that interferes with communication. The ideal is a perfect connection between your ideas and the reader's brain.

Failure to Write Grammatically

This impediment to understandability is just like the first one—mostly cosmetic. Grammar and spelling seldom have any effect on the reader's understanding of the literal meaning, but they have everything to do with how the reader receives the message. Consider this example:

> This here company hasn't issued no stock and hasn't got no plans to niether. When the owner's sell stock, they loose control, and this effects the companies operations. You keep doing what your doing in your company, this is the way we run our's.

The 12 grammatical errors here don't in any way keep you from knowing what the writer means; his meaning is so absolutely clear nobody could mistake it. But any reader would conclude that the owners are stupid and uneducated and that the company has a limited future. Whether such a conclusion is justified or not (and it isn't) is beside the point: by flagrantly disregarding all the rules of writing, the writer has produced all the wrong reactions from the reader.

On this point then, as on the first one, the lesson is simple: if you want your reader to take your work seriously, you must make it look as though you took it seriously too.

Failure to Write Appropriately and Effectively

Remember that writing never exists without an audience: you always write to somebody. If you inaccurately assess the person you're writing to, you create an impediment to understandability. Writing inappropriately—for instance, too formally, too informally, too technically, too simply, too humorously—can keep your reader from receiving the message the way you want it received.

Notice the different effects produced by these two memos:

Commencing on the first day subsequent to this memorandum, the undersigned will no longer partake of the midday meal in company with his hitherto accustomed associates, as a result of the assignment of new duties entailing a new and different time allotment.
 	
              Charles W. Nerf
	Joe—
	Sorry I won't be able to go to lunch with you from now on. Added work, different schedule.
	
	              Chuck

Neither of these is "wrong" in the abstract; each of them is appropriate for a different circumstance. If you're writing a note to the guy in the next office, it shouldn't sound like the Declaration of Independence, or it will be taken as something of much greater momentousness than you ever intended.

Rules for writing effectively, on the other hand, are pretty much the same for everybody. For instance, it is less effective to say "There are three obstacles to be overcome that the company is going to face in the future which lies ahead" than it is to say "The company faces three future obstacles." Things like conciseness, preciseness, forcefulness, and fluency are what make writing effective.

For these reasons the next two sections—the first on organized paragraphs and the second on strong sentences and clear style—are worth your closest attention.

ORGANIZED PARAGRAPHS

A paragraph is a unit of thought, not of length. It makes a point, a point different from what the previous paragraph made and different from what the next one will make.

In reader-friendly reports, paragraphs make their points directly and clearly, not indirectly, deviously, or subtly. Compare these two:

Bad	**Good**
When Mr. Fnerp became president of the Schlerg Company back in 2005, sales were $1.1 million. The kind of job he is doing is evident by noticing that they are now $725,000. The debt-equity ratio last year was 8:1. *Forbes* says the stock is overpriced. The financial condition of the company would not exactly be called very good.	The condition of the Schlerg Company is poor in every respect: stock price, debt, and sales. *Forbes* singled Schlerg out recently as an example of overpriced stock. Debt has mounted to the point where it is eight times equity. And sales have declined from $1.1 million to $725,000 in less than a decade. Nothing favorable can be said about the company's finances.

In the bad paragraph the reader has no idea till the end what the point is. At first we might think it's an account of Mr. Fnerp's work; then we might think it's a discussion of declining sales; then maybe something about current news. We have to grope our way through these first three sentences, wondering all the time why the writer is telling us these facts. But in the good paragraph, by contrast, the point—that the company is in rotten financial shape—is clear from the very first, and the facts plainly exist for the purpose of supporting, demonstrating, and proving this general point.

The good paragraph above is constructed in the classic four-part form:

1. **Say it**
2. **Explain it**
3. **Detail it**
4. **Say it again**

Look at each part in detail:

Say it	The condition of the Schlerg Company is poor in every respect:
Explain it	stock price, debt, and sales.
Detail it	1. *Forbes* magazine singled Schlerg out recently as an example of overpriced stock.
	2. Debt has mounted to the point where it is eight times equity.
	3. And sales have declined from $1.1 million to $725,000 in only a few years.
Say it again	Nothing favorable can be said about the company's finances.

This is (isn't it?) a pretty reasonable way of proceeding. Paragraph construction is a strategic question. You know something, and you have, by custom, only a certain amount of rectangular space in which to convince your readers that they should believe what you say. So to prepare your case logically, you should present the main conclusion at the first, make sure it's clear, provide the specifics to document it, and then remind your readers what the point is.

Look at it this way. If somebody said to you, "The Schlerg Company is in awful financial shape," you might reasonably ask for an explanation — "How so?" Your informant would then explain: "Stock, debt, and sales." Being an inquiring person, you would ask for details about each, which your informant would provide. Then, to make sure you haven't forgotten what the discussion was all about, your informant would remind you: "Nothing good can be said about the company's finances." Your informant has thus **said it**, **explained it**, **detailed it**, and **said it again**. Wow! Simple!

Now practice with a few other examples.

Practice: Identifying the Parts of a Well-Constructed Paragraph

Thinking of the say/explain/detail/say-again pattern can help not only in writing paragraphs but in reading them too. For practice, read each of these paragraphs, and note the **say it**, **explain it**, **detail it**, and **say it again** parts.

Paragraph 1

Recently the federal government has decided to implement several financial reporting reforms in	*Say it*
an effort to make it easier for shareholders to determine how much CEOs are getting paid and to understand the rationale for the compensation. Stock options,	*Explain it: amount and rationale*
which used to account for less than one-seventh of executive pay, have risen to one-third today, and since	*Detail it:*
companies were not required in the past to say how much these options are worth, investors have not been able to tell how much the executives are being compensated. The new rules require not only that the value must be plainly stated but also that any change in a CEO's pay	*(1) Amount*
over the years must be compared with changes in the company's performance, and that discrepancies between these two changes must be explained in writing.	*(2) Rationale*
Shareholder activists view these new regulations as a victory and a sign that more reforms may lie ahead.	*Say it again*

Paragraph 2

Sometimes the differences in production costs that companies experience in different locations can intensify rivalries between nations. That's what happened when the Japanese discovered it was cheaper to	*Say and explain— differences lead to rivalries*

produce Europe-bound products in the
United States or the United Kingdom than
at home. Ricoh now assembles photocopiers,   *Difference 1*
containing 90 percent Japanese parts, in California
and re-exports them to Europe. Sony produces   *Difference 2*
audiotapes and videotapes in Alabama, and
audiorecorders in Florida, and ships them to
Europe for sale. Other Japanese companies   *Difference 3*
have adopted locations in the United Kingdom
as their preferred manufacturing site for
products to be sold on the continent. As a
result, both the U.S. and the U.K. have become   *Resulting rivalries*
embroiled in disputes with the governments of
France, Germany, Spain, and Italy about exactly
what is meant by "Made in Japan," "Made in the
United States," and "Made in the United Kingdom."
Reduced-tariff agreements exist among some of these   *Say it again*
nations but not among others, and thus such definitions
make a difference.

Paragraph 3

When I left northeastern Ohio in 1962, it was   *Say it*
considered obvious and unquestionable that
Cleveland was well on its way to becoming one   *No explain-it needed*
of America's finest cities. Mayor Anthony
Celebrezze had just been invited to join   *Detail 1*
President Kennedy's cabinet as Secretary of
Health, Education, and Welfare. The St. Lawrence   *Detail 2*
Seaway had just opened, permitting huge freighters
from Europe to bring trans-Atlantic shipments all the
way to Cleveland. Western Reserve University and the   *Detail 3*
Case Institute of Technology, two distinguished universities,

were getting ready to merge into an even more
distinguished one. Finally, the Cleveland Museum   *Detail 4*
of Art was achieving national recognition for its
fine collections, and the great Cleveland Orchestra   *Detail 5*
was featured on the cover of *Time* magazine. Even
the Cleveland Indians and the Cleveland Browns   *Detail 6*
were doing well. Nothing that any of us could see
at the time would have led us to predict that in just   *Say it again,*
10 years Cleveland would have become one of   *with a twist*
America's worst examples of urban decay.

Now instead of just identifying parts, try your hand at putting them in the right order. Here are two disassembled paragraphs that need reassembling.

Practice: Reconstructing a Paragraph

Put these six sentences into the correct order so that they constitute a well-structured paragraph.

(A) Although still doing a brisk business at present, beer can producers will soon find their product being replaced by plastic bottles.

(B) Beer can production has been growing at more than 5 percent a year for at least 15 years, and cans now have 62.8 percent of the beer container market.

(C) The beer can industry appears to be in for bad times over the next decade.

(D) Cans will decline 3.5 percent annually until their market share dwindles to 30 percent in the next seven years.

(E) The forecasts clearly show that beer can production is a very poor prospect for new entrants into the industry and suggest that anyone interested in obtaining a share of the market would do well to look at plastic containers instead.

(F) Plastic beer bottles, which now have just 2.5 percent of the market, are expected to grow to 50 percent in the next 10 years.

Answer is given on the next page.

Answer

The beer can industry appears to be in for   *Say it: (C)*
bad times over the next decade. Although
still doing a brisk business at present,
beer can producers will soon find their   *Explain it: (A)*
product being replaced by plastic bottles.
Beer can production has been growing at   *Detail 1: (B)*
more than 5 percent a year for at least 15 years,
and cans now have 62.8 percent of the beer
container market. But cans will decline   *Detail 2: (D)*
3.5 percent annually until their market share
dwindles to 30 percent in the next seven years
Plastic beer bottles, which now have just   *Detail 3: (F)*
2.5 percent of the market, are expected to grow
to 50 percent in the next 10 years. Thus the   *Say it again: (E)*
forecasts clearly show that beer can production
is a very poor prospect for new entrants
into the industry and suggest that anyone
interested in obtaining a share of the market
would do well to look at plastic containers instead.

Okay, here's another one:

Put these five sentences into the correct order so that they form a well-structured paragraph.

(A) Steel, television sets, and VCRs are among the many products that will greatly benefit from the yen's appreciation as South Korea and others chip away at Japan's market share in these areas.

(B) While the yen has strengthened substantially, the currencies of Japan's Asian neighbors have been relatively steady against the dollar.

(C) South Korea's international competitive position has been particularly enhanced by the yen's rise, as evidenced by the 19.5 percent increase in exports recorded during the first two months of this year.

(D) Heightened sales competition from such newly industrialized countries of Asia as South Korea, Singapore, and Taiwan is clouding Japan's export outlook.

(E) Both the South Korean won and the Taiwan dollar have risen only slightly against the U.S. currency since the turn of the year, and the Singapore dollar has actually eased modestly.

Answer is given on the next page.

Heightened sales competition from such — Say it: (D)
newly industrialized countries of Asia
as South Korea, Singapore, and Taiwan is
clouding Japan's export outlook.

While the yen has strengthened — Explain it: (B)
substantially, the currencies of
Japan's Asian neighbors have been
relatively steady against the dollar.

Both the South Korean won and the Taiwan — Detail 1: (E)
dollar have risen only slightly
against the U.S. currency since the
turn of the year, and the Singapore
dollar has actually eased modestly.

South Korea's international competitive — Detail 2: (C)
position has been particularly
enhanced by the yen's rise, as
evidenced by the 19.5 percent
increase in exports recorded during
the first two months of this year.

Steel, television sets, and VCRs — Say it again: (A)
are among the many products that
will greatly benefit from the yen's
appreciation as South Korea and others
chip away at Japan's market share
in these areas.

Finally, here are two genuine student-written paragraphs. They are weak because the students who wrote them didn't structure them well, or maybe didn't structure them at all. Read them, and the marginal annotations, and then redesign them so that they are effectively structured.

The Paragraph

On the basis of profits five years ago,
the CEO of Consumers Union
began several new pro-consumer
ventures, including two new advocacy
offices, a children's magazine, syndicated
columns, and cable TV programs. These
efforts either lost money or broke even
and are the major cause of the current
deficit. The CEO sincerely believes
in consumer advocacy. This belief has,
in part at least, been responsible for
CU's reluctance to raise prices. Another
example of CU's heart was its delay in
closing an inefficient subscription
processing plant because it didn't want
to lay off so many employees. It is
possible that CU would not have the
operating deficit it does now, had the
move been made earlier.

The Reader's Reactions

[Ah, yes! The paragraph will discuss the four new ventures, one by one.]

[Lost money? Broke even? Deficit? Oh well—maybe it will tell about the financing of the new ventures.]

[Whoa—hold on. Advocacy? Not raising prices? Now I'm not sure what the point was.]

[Heart?? and a subscription plant?? I give positively up. What the hell was your point anyhow? Why have you been telling me all these things?]

Answer is given on the next page.

Answer

Suggested revision:

The basic cause of Consumers Union's troubles is that it   *Say it*
has allowed its concern for consumers to interfere with
sound business practices—in new ventures, unrealistically   *Explain it*
low prices, and inefficient operations. The new ventures
consisted of advocacy offices, a children's magazine,   *Detail 1*
syndicated columns, and a cable TV program. Even though
these ventures either lost money or only broke even, the
organization continued supporting them because they were
considered valuable services for consumers. The low cover   *Detail 2*
price for Consumer Reports *is another example. Although*
the magazine was losing money, the CEO kept its price low
so that the cost wouldn't be a burden to the readers. And
finally, a plant for processing subscriptions was kept open   *Detail 3*
even though the company knew it was inefficient, simply
because closing it would have meant laying off a number
of employees. If the company had paid more attention to
the business side of its operations, it probably would not   *Say it again*
be experiencing its current operating deficit.

The Paragraph	The Reader's Reactions
Consumers have a pessimistic attitude toward the use of paper goods. Generally people don't like to eat off paper plates. Plain white paper plates are most often purchased, so they are allotted the highest percentage of shelf space. However, the retail value of the plain plate is about one cent, which leaves little room for profit. Both consumers and supermarkets consider paper plates a summer commodity. Annual demands are low; therefore supermarkets bid every January for what is sold during the summer. This makes forecasting difficult and annual profits indeterminable.	*[It appears to be an analysis of consumer resistance to paper.]* *[Or maybe the subject is how to market paper to overcome the resistance?]* *[Or low profits? Hurry up and get it focused, will you? I'm getting sick of guessing.]* *[Maybe it was seasonality? Or forecasting? Oh come on—what was your point here anyway? Why have you been telling me all these things?]*

See how much corporate time a paragraph like this wastes? Somebody has gone to the trouble of researching and writing it, and all the people he's sent it to have gone to the trouble of reading it, but communication hasn't been moved forward even one inch, because nobody can tell what *point* it makes. Now look at the revised version to see how a transformation is brought about just by organizing clearly.

Answer is given on the next page.

Answer

Same paragraph, reorganized:

Nobody likes paper plates — not consumers, not retailers,	*Say it, and explain it*
not manufacturers. Consumers find eating off paper plates	*Detail 1*
to be an unpleasant and low-class experience. Retailers	*Detail 2*
dislike paper plates because they occupy a disproportionate	
amount of shelf space and bring little profit, only about a	
penny a package. And manufacturers dislike them because,	*Detail 3*
as seasonal products, they occupy the production machinery	
for only three months of the year and leave it to sit idle the	
rest of the time. Thus from every point of view, the paper	*Say it again*
plate industry is an unattractive one, and we should stay	
away from it.	

One more note here: Notice in all these examples that say-it isn't the same thing as say-it-again. When you say it, you're telling it to an uneducated audience, one that didn't know the point that you're making, so you just state the fact. But when you say it again, you're putting all the pieces together and showing how they relate to one another. It's not just a matter of repeating your first sentence at the end of the paragraph — in fact it's really irritating when people do that. Instead, you're summarizing, putting it all in perspective, and leading on to the next point.

We go now to sentences. No matter how great your ideas, how brilliant your organization, how well crafted your paragraphs, if your sentences stink, your report stinks.

STRONG SENTENCES AND CLEAR STYLE

The Nature of Grammar and Dictionaries

Before getting to the actual rules and suggestions, let us pause a moment to say something about the nature of "correctness" in language. Practically nobody today (other than linguistics experts) seems to understand anything about grammar—what it is, where it came from, what it's for, and so on. So this section will begin by clarifying a few points.

- **Grammar rules are not legislated.** There's no committee in the sky that decides what is or isn't correct.
- **Grammar rules are not fixed or permanent.** They apply differently in different circumstances and continuously change over time.
- **Grammar rules do not reflect "the way things used to be."** There never was a golden age when the language was "pure," an age from which we have sinfully declined and to which we must strive to restore ourselves. The traditional grammar rules that were taught in the schools for most of the last 200 years weren't even invented until the eighteenth century, just before the American Revolution, and even then they didn't reflect the past at all. They were just some people's ideas of what a noble language "should" be, based mostly on Latin, the language of ancient Rome.
- **Grammar rules do not have anything to do with clearer and more precise communication.** "This would be a nice town to live in" is at least as clear as "This would be a nice town in which to live." "I'll show you how to legally avoid paying taxes" is much clearer and more natural than "I'll show

you how legally to avoid paying taxes." Look how one author tortured his sentence to avoid splitting an infinitive:

Traditionally "Correct" but Hideously Awkward	Traditionally "Incorrect" but Much Better
In making a translation the first essential is thoroughly to understand what one is translating.	In making a translation the first essential is to thoroughly understand what one is translating.

Surely "Who are you talking about?" communicates a lot better than "About whom are you talking?" Even unacceptable things like "He don't hardly got none" are entirely clear in their literal meaning. In short, whatever those traditional grammar rules were supposed to accomplish, it wasn't clarity or precision.

■ **Dictionary makers are not lawgivers who decide what's right and what's wrong.** A dictionary is just a snapshot of the language at the time of publication. All sorts of new words and new meanings appear in each new dictionary, while old words and meanings are dropped. The reason is simply that people have started using the new words and meanings and stopped using the old ones. Nobody has used the very useful verbs *to inspissate* or *to oint* for more than a century, so those words never appear in dictionaries now, but those omissions don't mean the words are "wrong." *Decimate* used to mean "to reduce something by one-tenth," but people now use it to mean "to reduce something to just one-tenth of what it was," or in effect "to destroy," so that meaning is given in all modern dictionaries. Lots of words—*meat, prove, reek, nice, bolt, egregious*—have changed their meanings over the years, sometimes to exactly the opposite of what they used to mean. Words like *discombobulate*, with hardly any history behind them, entered dictionaries only a couple of decades ago and are now everywhere. Any dictionary that doesn't tell about new words and new meanings isn't doing its job: to portray what a language's words mean. Dictionaries don't decide—they report.

- **But nonetheless, grammar still exists, and certain ways of saying things are acceptable while others aren't.** In the 1960s a sort of "free speech" movement got started, in which it was argued that any way of saying something is just as good as any other way. We have pretty much outgrown that idea by now. If you were to find in your newspaper the statement "This here Middle East situation ain't getting no better," you would be appalled, because such is not an acceptable way of writing (or speaking), even though you know exactly what it means. So some kinds of grammar rules do still exist. What's happened, mainly, is that some rules have caught on in the public imagination and thus have acquired a sort of "social" validity. Until just a few generations ago, for example, the word *ain't* was widely used, widely accepted, and always understood. But late nineteenth-century grammarians decided to wage war on it, and it soon became the mark of an uncouth person. So even though it's a useful word that has a real function in English, it's been essentially banned.

There's equally little understanding of where grammar came from. In its simplest form, the history of English grammar can be said to have had three phases:

1. *Traditional Latinate grammar (1700s to 1950s)*: Some eighteenth century writers and thinkers, noting that the civilization of ancient Rome was the greatest in the history of humankind, decided that the English language should be molded into the model of the noble Latin language, as the first step in making the modern civilization as great as the ancient one. The kind of tortured syntax that resulted—no prepositions at the ends of sentences, no split infinitives, confusing plurals like *indices* and *spectra*, awkward and pretentious phrases like *it is I, data are* and *I shall*, a ban on abbreviations and contractions—was what was taught in schools for two centuries. It gave rise to a lot of criticism and some parodies, but it wasn't really dislodged until the middle of the twentieth century.

2. *The structural linguistics movement (1940s to 1960s)*: Believing that we should have a grammar system based on our own language rather than on a foreign one, a group of scholars undertook to break from the traditional model and create a new one that would be *descriptive* rather than *prescriptive*—that would fit the language rather than try to force the language to fit the grammar. Instead of being based on Latin and telling you what you *should* say, it was based on actual usage, that is, on what people *really do* say: if you've heard it or seen it, in other words, then it's acceptable English. They called their model "structural linguistics," and it was the rage for about 20 years, starting around the late 1940s, even making its way into school curriculums for a few years.

3. *Transformational generative syntax*: In 1957 linguist Noam Chomsky wrote a short book in which he demonstrated that usage isn't what determines "correctness"—that nonsensical sentences you would never hear can be entirely good English while some perfectly clear but unidiomatic statements can be wrong even if a million people say them. He proposed instead a new system of grammar that shows how a language transforms meanings ("deep structures") into sentences ("surface structures"). It's an elegant system, but, as Chomsky points out, it has absolutely no practical application—it doesn't help in learning a language, in teaching a language, or in checking one's own language for "correctness."

Thus, although we know that some things are acceptable English and some aren't, we have no comprehensive grammatical system to explain why. As a result, schools stopped teaching "grammar" about 40 years ago. They were correct to do so. The subject matter is far more important than the language that conveys it.

Nonetheless, a difference between "good writing" and "bad writing" still exists, and that's the reason for these next few pages.

Fourteen Sentence Rules

Compare these two passages:

Bad

There were 11 people in attendance at the meeting. Nine of these 11 people were in agreement concerning the hiring of additional secretarial assistance. The other two were hesitant, expressing a preference for a continuation of the present policy of being reliant upon their existing staffing.

Good

Of the 11 people at the meeting, nine favored hiring more secretaries. The other two hesitated, saying they preferred to rely on their present staff.

Both these passages are "correct," since they don't violate any grammar rules, but the one on the right is far better because its sentences are more vigorous and more efficient. The difference becomes even more marked in longer reports: if you had to read 10 pages instead of just one paragraph, you would find yourself getting worn down, bored, and lulled to sleep by the kind of writing on the left.

Following is a checklist of 14 rules that you can follow to make your sentences strong. But remember that "rules" in writing are mostly just suggestions. Don't obey any of these rules if the result sounds bad.

Rule 1. When You Can, Use Real Verbs in Preference to Be Verbs

"I favor" rather than "I am in favor of"; "I believe" rather than "I am of the belief that"; "it benefits" rather than "it is beneficial to"; "we depend on" rather than "we are dependent on." *Rely* is a real verb; *are reliant* isn't.

Look at the verbs in your sentences. When you have a *be* verb (*am, are, is, was, were, has been, have been*), see if you can change it to a real verb—that is, an action verb, in which somebody does something instead of just being something. You can't always, of course. But if more than half your verbs are *be* verbs, you haven't tried hard enough.

Here are some examples:

Instead Of	Use
We are in agreement with	We agree with
We are in receipt of	We have received
We are of the opinion that	We think
This is the result of	This results from
This is illustrative of	This illustrates

Rule 2. Avoid -*tion* Words Where Possible

Almost all -*tion* words (*organization, production, coordination*) used to be verbs (*organize, produce, coordinate*). In their -*tion* form, however, they are only stifled, strangled, smothered ex-verbs—lifeless hulks, verbs that have lost their verbhood. Compare these two sentences:

Bad	Good
The motivation of his actions is the desire for recognition.	He acts as he does because he wants people to notice him.

In the weak sentence on the left, the active ideas (motivate! act! desire! recognize!) are mostly suffocating in -*tion* forms, while the word that should convey the action—the verb—is only a crummy little *is*. The sentence on the right is far better because it uses active word forms for active words. Especially if you had to read several pages of each kind of writing, you would realize how much can be achieved by liberating ex-verbs from their noun-shackles and restoring them to their rightful roles as the active elements in the sentences.

Rule 3. Avoid the Passive Voice Where Possible

Almost all real verbs can be active or passive. In the active voice, the subject does something: "We bought the stock." In the passive voice, on the other hand, something is done to the subject: "The stock was bought by us." Both are "correct," of course, but after a few paragraphs the passive begins to sound sickly.

Check to see if your passives are convertible to actives. You'll recognize passive verbs because they consist of *be* (i.e., *am, are, is, was, were, has been, have been*) plus the participle: *am apprised, are requested, is desired, was decided, were mailed, has been sent, have been programmed.*

Passive	Active
Action will be taken after the decision has been announced by the committee.	We will act after the committee has announced its decision.
This question will be decided by the president.	The president will decide this question.

You can't always use active verbs instead of passive ones—but when you can, do. Can you imagine Rhett Butler saying, "Frankly, my dear, a damn is not given by me"?

Rule 4. When You Can Do So, Avoid *There Is* and *There Are*

There doesn't mean anything. If somebody says "There are three things," you can't even say "Where?" *There* simply announces the existence of something, and it's usually not necessary to do that.

Compare these two sentences:

Bad	Good
There were three things that caused the company to fail.	Three things caused the company to fail.

The one on the right is stronger because it directs the reader's thoughts: "There are three things" doesn't lead anywhere, but "Three things caused" points straight in the direction you want your reader to go.

Check to see if your *there is* and *there are* phrases (also there was, *there were, there has been, there have been, there will be*) can be easily replaced by more active and efficient phrases. If so, do it.

Rule 5. Subordinate Less-Important Elements

Not all things in a sentence are equally important. A well-written sentence reflects such differences by expressing the more important idea as the main part of the sentence and the subordinate idea as a subordinate element—something less important, grammatically, than a complete sentence.

Look for instance at these two:

Bad	Good
I have been studying this company for years, and it is slowly going broke.	This company, which I have been studying for years, is slowly going broke.

Clearly the important point is that the company is going broke. The sentence on the right indicates this emphasis by subordinating the less important point to a less important grammatical form—a mere *which* clause—thus signaling to the reader what the major point is.

Here's another example:

Bad	Good
This report has been in management's hands only a few days, and it will change the entire marketing strategy.	This report, which has been in management's hands only a few days, will change the entire marketing strategy.

Look at your sentences and see if you can distinguish some main ideas from some lesser ones; then try to put the lesser ones in lesser grammatical forms. Following this rule can do wonders in making your writing vigorous and unmistakably clear, because it focuses the reader's attention on the important points.

Rule 6. Eliminate All Unimportant Elements

Over the past few decades, people have started including irrelevant things—like "over the past few decades"—in their sentences. (Just think about it and you'll immediately see how irrelevant that phrase was! What difference could the length of time possibly make?) Getting rid of such irrelevancies isn't easy, since it's hard to identify them in your own writing. The secret lies in aiming for the jugular vein—in thinking carefully about precisely what the sentence is supposed to say and then striking away anything that's extra. Examine these:

Bad	Good
Since I came to work at Schlerg Company six months ago, at least 10 people have told me that the research laboratories are off limits to office and administrative personnel. Is this true?	Are research laboratories off limits to office and administrative personnel?

Clearly the length of the writer's service at Schlerg hasn't got anything to do with the question; neither has the number of people who said the areas are off limits. By taking out both those extraneous pieces of information, the writer makes the sentence direct, uncluttered, and consequently clear.

Have another example:

Bad	Good
We have examined the research findings of all previous investigators in this area and have found that none of them seems to have reached any significant conclusions regarding the cause of the leakage.	Previous research has not identified the cause of the leakage.

Look how many irrelevant things were hiding in that seemingly normal sentence: "we have examined," "findings," "previous investigators," "seems to have," "significant," and more. Without them, the sentence is stunningly clearer.

Rule 7. Be Sure *This*, *That*, and *Which* Refer to Something Specific

Although the writer usually knows what *this* means, the reader often doesn't. Look, for instance, at this sentence:

Unclear	**Clear**
John said he was told that the treasurer believes stock options will improve employee motivation, but this is not true.	John said he was told that the treasurer believes stock options will improve employee motivation, but whoever told him such a thing must have been misinformed. The treasurer doesn't feel that way at all.

Depending on what *this* refers to, the original sentence could have meant that (1) John is lying—nobody told him any such thing, (2) the person who told John was wrong—the treasurer doesn't believe any such thing, or simply (3) stock options won't improve employee motivation. It was impossible to tell which one the writer meant.

Even more common than such ambiguity is simple vagueness. Try this one:

Recent developments have led economists to rethink many of their most basic assumptions. If full employment and low inflation can exist simultaneously, then the implications for such social programs as unemployment insurance and job training are staggering. This suggests . . .

This? THIS?? "This" has nothing to refer to. The rethinking? The simultaneous existence of high employment and low inflation? The social implications? Actually, none of these answers is satisfactory. Probably the author means something about new economics, but this—to illustrate the point—is not enough. Say "this belief," "this plan," "this turmoil," or something similar so that your reader knows exactly what you're referring to.

Rule 8. Avoid Clichés

We all have a tendency to gravitate toward standard, "automatic" phrases. Don't. Instead of enhancing our writing and speaking, such phrases usually serve as substitutes for thought. We get much more out of being told that something is practically worthless than out of being told that it's "a dime a dozen." And notice how much clearer it is to say that older employees may have trouble with technology than it is to say "You can't teach an old dog new tricks."

Moreover, sometimes such phrases get tangled up with one another, as in a magazine report that "Floods are exploding across the midwest," a board member's statement that "The president has a dark horse up his sleeve," or a company newspaper's statement that "There are many new faces to fill the shoes of recent retirees." Clearly, the people who wrote such sentences didn't think about what they were saying but instead used the automatic phrases as substitutes.

Recently, a new generation of very irritating clichés has sprung up. Before you say "think outside the box," "level the playing field," "mixing apples and oranges," "not rocket science (or brain surgery)," "reinvent the wheel," "talk the talk/walk the walk," or "push the envelope," see if you can make your point more effectively without resorting to such tired phrases.

Rule 9. Don't Overqualify

Don't say "I would agree" if you really mean "I agree." Don't say "It would seem" when you mean "It seems." Don't say "The company may perhaps appear to be in some degree of trouble" when you mean "Bail out! The company is up to its armpits in lawsuits!"

Overqualifying has become rampant in business writing. People say "It would appear that the company may be in some trouble" when they mean "It appears that the company is in some trouble." And they say "It appears that the company is in some trouble" when they mean "The company is in some trouble," or, more likely, "The company is in trouble."

Such overcautiousness is cowardly and potentially misleading. In any case, it doesn't do any good, since it doesn't fool anybody and wouldn't be enough to prevent somebody from suing you. Most of the time it's just a bad habit.

Especially be careful to use *would* only in an *if* situation. "I would agree" ought to mean "I would agree IF certain conditions existed, but as it is I don't." Likewise, "The company would seem to be in trouble" ought to mean "The company doesn't seem to be in trouble." Avoid the ambiguity. If you think something or recommend something, say that you think it or recommend it, not that you "would."

Rule 10. Be Parallel—Same Form for Same Function

When you make a list of things, even of just two things, put the items in the same form. If one is a command (for example, "Increase advertising expenditures") then the next must also be a command ("Construct a new building") rather than some other form such as "Construction of a new building." Look at this really-hard-to-read sentence and its corrected versions:

Bad	**Good**
Our objectives this year are to grow, diversification, and that we improve service.	Our objectives this year are to grow, to diversify, and to improve service.

OR   Our objectives this year
are growth, diversification,
and improved service.

OR   Growing, diversifying, and
improving service are our
objectives this year.

If one is an *-ing,* then all must be *-ings.* Otherwise your list is really hard to read.

Parallelism is especially a problem in sentences where three items that don't actually belong in the same list are put together:

Bad	Good
We sell stationery, office supplies, and are considering selling computers.	We sell stationery and office supplies and are considering selling computers.

"Stationery," (2) "office supplies," and (3) "are considering"???? Obviously the third one of these doesn't belong in the same list as the first two. The solution here is to make two lists—(1) things we do (we *sell* and we *are considering*) and (2) things we sell (*stationery* and *office supplies*).

This problem really shows up in PowerPoint presentation slides. When you present a list of things to an audience, be sure all the items are in the same form.

Rule 11. Use the Simplest, Toughest Words Possible

English, being a sloppy mixture of Germanish and Frenchish, has two words for everything—a tough German-like one and a more dandified Frenchy-Latiny one. Examples are *dog/canine, guts/intestines, eat/ingest,* and *puke/vomit*. Two entirely correct English sentences thus can produce two different effects:

Following mastication and ingestion of a despoliated deceased feline, the canine regurgitated the contents of its intestines in the exterior edifice.	After chewing up and eating a rotten dead cat, the dog puked up everything from its guts in the outhouse.

Of course you can't, despite the temptation, say "puke" in a business report; but you can say "dog" instead of "canine," "house" instead of "domicile," and "dried" instead of "desiccated." And you should: using the tougher and more common word will make your writing much more readable.

Here are some others:

Instead Of	Say
expedite, accelerate	speed up
attempt, endeavor	try
facilitate	make easier
assist	help
adhere	stick
disintegrate	crumble
utilize	use
desiccated	dry
deceased	dead
elevated	high
animated	lively
circular	round
tripartite	three-part
conflagration	fire
illumination	light
edifice	building
implement	tool
carton	box
valise	bag

Phony attempts to sound profoundly learned by using fancy Latin words merely cause a reader to become thoroughly micturated.

Rule 12. Use Specific Rather Than General Words

Don't begin your report by saying you "will discuss certain recent developments"; nobody will have any idea what you mean. It's appalling how often writers retreat into abstractions like that. Probably they think it's a good way to introduce a subject, but they're wrong. It's dumb.

Look how little is communicated when you tell your reader "The following may be of interest to you" or "We thought you ought to be informed about some recent activities." Getting quickly to the point is important, and using specific words — what activities? what developments? why will it interest me? — is a good way to do it.

Do not say "development" when you mean "unfortunate episode," or "unfortunate episode" when you mean "deaths," or "deaths" when you mean "sniper killings."

Can you tell what this statement means? "We must take steps to assure preparedness in the event of necessity." It could (couldn't it?) refer to almost anything, even something like setting up a cocktail party. Actually it came from a homeland security instruction pamphlet, and it creates a nuclear cloud of doubt about the effectiveness of the Homeland Security Department's work.

Rule 13. Vary the Length and Pattern of Your Sentences

The monotonous droning rhythm generated by sentences that all are the same length and that all start with the subject can be broken up simply by varying the length and the pattern. Compare these two paragraphs: the facts they present are the same, but the one on the left is a bore and the one on the right is interesting.

Bad

Complaints about office conditions have been received. Window leakage is a serious problem. Rain seeps in all the windows during storms. Lack of heat in the winter is also serious. The ventilation system does not work well. Several workers have requested transfers to other buildings.

Good

We have received many complaints about office conditions. One concerns the windows: each time it rains, water seeps in at every one of them. Other complaints concern the lack of heat in winter and the inadequate ventilation all year long. As a result of such problems, employees have started requesting transfers to other buildings.

Stay alert for this problem. You can make your sentences different from one another, and thereby avoid the droning problem, simply by writing a long one followed by a short one, and by starting them with verbs and adverbs and various kinds of introductions and inversions rather than always with the subject. You never need sound like a preacher again.

Rule 14. Have Somebody Read Your Report Aloud to You

When you read your own report, you can make it sound exactly the way you wanted it to sound when you wrote it. But when somebody else reads it to you, then you hear it the way it sounds to a reader. The experience can be really enlightening.

Ask someone who has never read your report before, even silently, to read it aloud to you. If possible, keep a recorder on while the person is reading, so you can listen to it again and again.

Listen for awkward places that make your reader stumble, or for unexpected rhymes or other distractions, or for places that don't bring out the emphasis you want. Don't underestimate the value of this experience—the ultimate safety device for assuring that your report sounds professional.

Twelve Other Stylistic Considerations

In addition to those 14 sentence rules, here are another 12 general suggestions about how to handle some frequently occurring problems in order to make your style readable and to avoid irritating your reader.

1. *Me, Myself*, and *I*

All those years of having traditional English teachers insist that people say "It is I" have led whole generations to think that *I* is somehow a superior word to *me*. It isn't, of course. Hearing people pretentiously say *I* when they should say *me* is really irritating. Most of the time the problem occurs when the sentence says something like "somebody else and I," as in "Make an appointment with either my assistant or [I, me]" and "They invited my wife and [I, me] to the party." The secret to telling which one is correct in these instances is just to drop the "somebody else" and say only "I"—you'll instantly hear which one is right. Thus the following are all correct:

Make an appointment with either Dr. Hudeili or me.   ("with me")
Tell this to either my secretary or me.   ("to me")
This is just between you and me.   ("between me")
Please keep Charles and me informed.   ("keep me")
They invited Anita and me to dinner.   ("invited me")
At least three people will be here—Bill, Nancy, and I. ("I will be here")
They should honor faithful employees like Joe and me. ("like me")

Many people try to avoid the problem by saying "myself," as in "My associates and myself will be glad to help you." That's simply another irritation.

2. *Who* and *Whom*

The old-fashioned rules for *who* and *whom* did in fact make sense, but trying to explain them to people who've never had to study grammar is close to impossible. Maybe the answer is just to say what sounds good, without thinking about which way is probably "correct." Thus it sounds okay to say "Who did you tell that to?" even though you'd probably say "You told that to whom?" You would probably find it natural to say "Who should I congratulate?" even though the traditional rule would call for "whom." Under traditional grammar rules it's a double standard, but nobody cares. Sometimes either one sounds good, and so you have a choice—"The person who I choose will serve for two years" or "The person whom I choose will serve for two years." Officially it's "whom," but nobody will notice. (And just to show how hard it is to explain, note that the traditional rules would require you to say "Whoever I choose will serve for two years.") To say it again, the best course of action is to forget about what you think is "correct" and just say what sounds good. Normally you'll say "who." In the few instances where that sounds awful, say "whom."

3. What to Do When English Lacks a Word

Sometimes when the problem lies with the language, you just have to use a longer phrase to avoid sounding moronic.

We say "He did, didn't he?" and "You are, aren't you?" But what about "I am, _____ I?" Lacking a word "amn't," and forbidden to say "ain't," and not wanting to sound pretentious by saying "am I not?" some people say "aren't I," but that's a really low-class uncouth thing to say. So you have to go around a longer route and say something like "I am, don't you think?"

Similarly, we say "people *whose* wealth is over a million" and "the man *whose* car this is," but we don't have a similar word for *things*: how do you say "Any company _____'s sales have risen"? Lacking a word like "which's," we again have to take a longer route and say "Any company that experienced rising sales," or something similar. Don't say "the company whose"—irritating.

And one more: Except for southerners who say "you-all" and a few New Yorkers who still say "youse," English has no way of distinguishing between one of you and many of you. "Did you find any problems with the contract?" could mean either did the specific person you're talking to or did anybody in the whole company. So again, to avoid ambiguity take a longer route: "Did anybody there find problems?" or "Did you yourself find any problems?"

4. *Which* and *That*

When you can say "that" instead of "which," do. It flows better.

5. *Different From* and *Different Than*

Than means "compared with," as in "bigger than," "richer than," "smarter than." *Different* is different. One thing differs *from* another, not *than* it. Khruschev was different *from* Stalin; Stalin was more ruthless *than* Khruschev. Trying to get people to say "different from" is probably a losing battle, but hearing or reading "different than" is a real irritation. It does sometimes take a few more words—"He does it differently than I do" would have to become "He does it differently from the way I do it." But the few extra words are worth the effort. *Different* means a *separation* between two kinds of things, not a *comparison* between them.

6. *Include* and *Including*

People often say "including" when they mean "consisting of." *Include* refers to a part, not to the whole thing. If your company makes six products, then those six might include shirts and neckties. But if it makes *only* those two products, then it's wrong to say that "it makes two products, including shirts and neckties." Instead you would need to say "It makes two products—shirts and neckties." Even worse, one now sometimes hears the phrase "some of these include." First of all, that's redundant—*some of* and *include* mean the same thing. But it also seems to make the nonsensical suggestion that *others* of these *don't* include. All you have to do is say "some of these are." Even better you can just put a colon after the thing that preceded, as in "She made a number of suggestions: enlarging the department, diversifying the product line, and increasing advertising."

7. Putting *Only* and *Not* in the Right Places

You shouldn't say "We only drove 50 miles," because you don't mean "only drove"—you mean "only 50." "The company only made three products" is imprecise; try "The company made only three products." The same principle applies to the use of "not." "Everybody is not satisfied" means something entirely different from "Not everybody is satisfied." Put "only" and "not" next to the word they belong with.

8. "One of Those Things That . . . [*Is* or *Are*?]"

Which is it?

The easiest way to explain it is to write a play. If the original statement said "Martino's is one of those companies that ____ in trouble," then the dialogue would go like this:

    A: Martino's is one.
    B: One what?
    A: One of those companies.
    B: What companies?
    A: Those companies that are in trouble.

Thus the answer is *are*. The statement places one item—Martino's—in a larger group. So Martino's is, but the companies are.

Of course it would be different if you said "Martino's is *the only one* of those companies that *is* in trouble," and different again if you said "Martino's is the only one of those companies that *are* in trouble that *is* doing something about it." But let's not get into all that. The point here is that normally the situation involves one item that *is* in a bigger group of things that *are* or *do* or *make* or *have*. "The First Presbyterian Church *is* one of those buildings that *have been* landmarked."

9. Keeping Track of the Subject in spite of a Long Interruption

When a sentence has a long separation between its subject and its verb, the writer or speaker can sometimes forget whether it was singular or plural. Here's one:

> The combination of three kinds of natural disasters (tornadoes, floods, earth-quakes), some serious economic setbacks during the past six months, and two lawsuits involving patents and discrimination charges [has? have?] made this a difficult year for us.

Clearly the right choice is "has," since the subject was "combination." Sometimes it helps to read your work aloud; you'll be more likely to remember the subject if you hear it instead of just see it.

10. Is a Company an *It* or a *They*?

Very simply, a company can be either *it* or *they*—but not both at the same time. Quite often people write "The company is very proud of its reputation, and they work hard to maintain it." That's wrong, of course, because it's inconsistent—the company was "it" in the first half of the sentence and "they" in the second half. It doesn't really irritate (or not much anyway) for somebody to say "the company is proud of their reputation," even though "is" means it's singular and "their" means it's plural. Most people can overlook that little problem. But when a writer has declared a company to be an "it" then it has to remain an "it," throughout.

Of course this whole discussion doesn't apply to Great Britain, where all companies are always plural: "Shell are," "London Transport are," "Sainsbury are." If the Americans similarly thought of companies as plural, that would solve the whole problem.

11. Slashes and Readabiliy

Writing that provides alternatives by the use of slashes is really hard to read. Instead of saying "banks/financial institutions" one should say "banks or financial institutions," and instead of "manufactures/sells" it should be "manufactures and sells." One problem with a slash is that it doesn't tell the reader whether you mean "or" or "and." But another problem is evident when you try to read the phrases aloud. "Banks financial institutions" and "manufactures sells" don't read right. In fact reading aloud is the key to many of the problems discussed here. Whatever is easiest to read aloud is normally the best way to write something.

12. *Data Is* or *Data Are*?

You can't win here. If you say "the data is," some people will cluck their tongues in haughty disapproval. If you say "the data are," others will wince at your silly pretentiousness.

The solution, therefore, is to use another word instead of "data." Say "the statistics are" or "the information is" and thereby sidestep the problem.

Historically, by the way, people have been saying "data is" for two centuries, and almost nobody said "data are" until some busybody grammarians began insisting on that usage. As is true of most other such questions, it's a myth to think of "the way it used to be." It never was.

SENTENCE CONNECTIVES

The whole point of writing well, as you may have figured out by now, is to make things easier for your readers. The ideal business report is one in which the readers, on just one reading, will fully understand everything you intended them to understand.

One of the surest ways of accomplishing that objective is to tell people in advance what they're getting ready to read. Experiments have repeatedly shown that the more you know in advance about what you're reading, the greater will be your speed and comprehension.

That's the reason for all the organizational things said so far—stating the conclusion plainly and straightforwardly at the first, and then telling what your reasons are and where the discussion of each can be found; using thesis-like subheadings or keywords to demarcate and introduce the segments; and following a logical order (say it, explain it, detail it, and say it again) within each segment. So I mean, like, you know, how clear can it get?

Answer: Would you believe, still clearer yet? Even your individual sentences can carry some sort of tagword to let the readers know in advance, before they read it, what it's going to say. Nobody should ever have to read a sentence twice or ever have to wonder what the point of any sentence is.

Suppose, for example, you have read a sentence saying "St. Louis is located on a river, and Trenton is located on a river." If the next sentence begins "Likewise, . . ." then you know just from that one beginning word what the rest of the sentence is going to tell you: the name of another river city. Likewise (see?) if you have read that "Virginia's population grew during the 1980s, as did Colorado's," and the next sentence begins "However, . . .," then you know that the next sentence will tell about a state that shrank.

Compare these two paragraphs for a demonstration of the value of connective or "signpost" words like *likewise* and *however*:

1. Disconnected

Schlerg has severe financial problems. Its stock is overpriced. The market value of the company is expected to fall soon. Sales revenues have declined in seven of the last eight years. Sales did increase by 15 percent in 1992. That was the year after the recession. The overall decline over the whole period is approximately 40 percent. The company's debt situation cannot be described as good. The debt-equity ratio is 8 to 1. Much of the debt is short term.

2. Connected

Schlerg has severe financial problems. *For instance*, its stock is over-priced, *and consequently* the market value of the company is expected to fall soon. *Furthermore* sales revenues have declined in seven of the last eight years. *Although* sales did increase 15 percent in 1992, the year after the recession, *still* the total decline over the whole period is approximately 40 percent. *Finally*, the company's debt situation cannot be described as good. *Specifically*, the debt-equity ratio is 8 to 1, *and* much of the debt is short term.

Following is a list of such signpost words, which have the effect of pointing your reader in the right direction for receiving the upcoming sentence. Search through your writing for places where you can advantageously use some of these—places where your paragraph is taking a turn, or giving an example, or adding another in a list of things. By using these words, you can make the reader's job fantastically easier.

If You Want Your Reader to Expect:	Then Use One of These Words:
More of the same	and, also, furthermore, moreover, additionally, in addition, likewise, similarly, plus, second (third . . . *n*th), next, finally

If You Want Your Reader to Expect:	Then Use One of These Words:
Something different	but, still, yet, nevertheless, nonetheless, however, on the other hand, though, although, even though, unlike, on the contrary, by contrast, in contrast
An illustration of what was just said	for example, for instance, specifically, such as, like, to illustrate, among them, one such, one of them, one
The result of what was just said	therefore, thus, consequently, as a result, as a consequence, so, hence, because of this
The cause of what was just said	because, due to, owing to, as a result of, as a consequence of
A restatement of what was just said	to repeat, to reiterate, to say it again, indeed, in fact, in other words, once again, in summary, to summarize, to sum up

Practice: Connecting Sentences with Signpost Words

The following two paragraphs, written by a student, at first seem confused, contradictory, and almost unintelligible. But they actually are excellently reasoned. All they lack is connectives. Supply them.

An internship program at Slert Corporation seems inappropriate. This successful company has experienced rapid growth. An evaluation of the corporate structure reveals many areas of internship opportunity. A history of illegal activities and poor employee relations precludes its selection. Socially beneficial charitable acts seem nonexistent. Better internship opportunities for both the student and the university exist elsewhere.

Workers at Slert Corporation have a long history of unhappiness. The company rewards productive management employees very well, with bonuses often exceeding salaries. The store managers' pay is based on incentive plans that are the most generous in retailing today. Turnover among managers of company-owned stores reached 52 percent three years ago. The company offers no retirement plan. Wages for its non-management employees are low, averaging two-thirds of those at comparable retail stores. Managers' hours and responsibilities are a problem.

Answer is given on the next page.

Answer

The same paragraphs with signpost words:

An internship program at Slert Corporation seems inappropriate. **Although** *this successful company has experienced rapid growth,* **and although** *an evaluation of the corporate structure reveals many areas of internship opportunity,* **nonetheless** *a history of illegal activities and poor employee relations precludes its selection.* **Furthermore,** *socially beneficial charitable acts seem nonexistent.* **Therefore,** *better internship opportunities for both the student and the university exist elsewhere.*

Workers at Slert Corporation have a long history of unhappiness. **Despite the fact that** *the company rewards productive management employees very well, with bonuses often exceeding salaries,* **and also the fact that** *the store managers' pay is based on incentive plans that are the most generous in retailing today,* **still** *turnover among managers of company-owned stores reached 52 percent three years ago.* **One reason is that** *the company offers no retirement plan.* **Another is that** *wages for its non-management employees are low, averaging two-thirds of those at comparable retail stores.* **And finally,** *managers' hours and responsibilities are a problem.*

NUMBERS AND WORDS

Since business reports regularly use numbers, a few rules about number-writing for maximum understandability have sprung up over the years.

Rule 1. Use words for 1-9, figures for 10 and up. "I own three cats and 35 shares of IBM."

Rule 2. Never, however, start a sentence with a figure. If a number larger than 9 comes at the beginning, use words. "Twenty-three weeks ago, Schlerg Company went out of business."

Rule 3. Very large numbers are usually best handled with a combination of figures and words: "$50 trillion," "6.62 billion people."

Rule 4. When using decimals like .2 and .66, always write "0.2" and "0.66," to avoid confusion. The same applies when you're speaking: say "zero point two" and "zero point sixty-six."

Rule 5. When using a fraction, follow Rule 1. Write "one-eighth," "eight and a half," and "18½."

Rule 6. Remember that readability is the criterion. If you still have a question about how to write a number, use the way that is easiest to read out loud.

Rule 7. Use *number* for things you can count, *amount* for a quantity or mass. A number of potatoes make an amount of mashed potatoes; a number of apples make an amount of applesauce; a number of dollars make an amount of money; a number of lawyers make an amount of trouble. Do not say "an amount of people" or "an amount of women" or "an amount of customers": they can be counted. The number of customers determines the amount of business.

Rule 8. Use *fewer* for things you can count, *less* for a quantity or mass. Fewer potatoes make less mashed potatoes; fewer apples make less applesauce; fewer lawyers make less trouble. "Fewer students," "fewer women," "fewer farmers and farms"; "less education," "less electoral power," "less farming."

Rule 9. A *number* are; *the number* is. A *number* is like *a lot*. "A number of factors are involved." "A number of tickets are still available, but the number of remaining tickets is growing smaller every day."

Rule 10. *Percent* may be spelled either *per cent* (British) or *percent* (American). When writing percents, use figures: 8 percent, 18 percent.

Rule 11. When discussing periods of time, if you use *from* then you must use *to*. You can say "during 2002-2008" but *not* "from 2002-2008." You have to say "from 2002 to 2008." Read aloud and you'll see why.

Rule 12. Remember that a number has *no significance whatever* unless it's compared with another number. Sales of $3.4 billion are good if last year's were just $2.7 billion but bad if last year's were $4.6 billion. A 3 percent increase in exports is good if other countries' exports increased by 2 percent, bad if other countries' exports increased by 4 percent. Is it good that the Schlerg Company operates in 25 countries? Well, if its chief competitors operate in 41 countries, then the answer is No—it's far behind the others. "My company's profits last year were 13 cents"—good or bad? If it's a lemonade stand that opened in a small town in northern Canada at 4 p.m. on December 31, this figure may represent an all-time industry high. *Every number must be compared to another number.*

POSSESSIVE APOSTROPHES

Apostrophes cause more trouble per square inch than any other punctuation mark. Why that should be is a mystery: the rules are simple, and, miracle of all miracles, they have no exceptions.

Since everything that can possess something is either singular or plural, and since every word either does or doesn't end in S or Z, this simple four-cell matrix includes all possibilities:

	Singular	Plural
Doesn't end in S or Z	's	's
Ends in S or Z	either ' or 's	'

Possibility 1. Upper Left Cell. A singular noun that doesn't end in S or Z: *dog, cat, IBM, Joe, company, economy, Britain.* Just add 's:

> The dog's tail, the cat's paw, IBM's reorganization, Joe's job, the company's plans, the economy's downturn, Britain's role in the European Community

Possibility 2. Lower Right Cell. A plural noun that does end in S or Z: *dogs, cats, bosses, countries*. Just add ':

> Five dogs' tails, three cats' owners, secretaries on their bosses' Christmas
> lists, the Asian countries' productivity

Possibility 3. Lower Left Cell. A singular noun that does end in S or Z: *Charles, boss, Onassis, bus, Rutgers*. Just add either ' or *'s*—take your pick:

> Charles' job or Charles's job, the boss' instructions or the boss's instructions,
> Onassis' fortune or Onassis's fortune, Rutgers' program or Rutgers's program

Either one is always right. The difference is only in the pronunciation: when you add *'s*, you add an extra syllable. Thus *Onassis'* is pronounced *Onassis*, and *Onassis's* is pronounced *Onassises*. *Rutgers'* is pronounced *Rutgers*, and *Rutgers's* is pronounced *Rutgerses*. Thus you probably would want to say "the boss's [pronounced *bosses*] instructions" but "Rutgers' [pronounced *Rutgers*] program" simply because they sound more normal that way. Either, however, is always acceptable.

Possibility 4. Upper Right Cell. A plural noun that doesn't end in S or Z: *men, women, children, alumni*. Just add *'s*:

> Men's clothing, women's rights, children's education, alumni's donations

Note: Never use apostrophes with possessive pronouns. Write *ours, yours, hers, theirs, whose, its*. The word *it's* isn't a possessive; it means "it is" or "it has." The word *its*, the possessive, means "belonging to it" or "characteristic of it":

> It's true that a dog wags its tail.

Practice: Possessive Apostrophes

Insert the correct form in each blank.

When a _____ profit margin starts to dwindle,
   company

or when the profit margin of one of its _____
                                          subsidiaries

does, then it's time to call on one of the business _____
                                                    world

multitude of consulting firms. Let us recommend _____.
                                                 ours

We have an accounting staff _____ training amounts to
                            who

over 125 _____ of service, and _____ is a quality
         year   their

hard to equal. Our _____ duty is to spend all
                   experts

their time and effort solving the problems of the _____
                                                  country

leading _____. We think of these _____
        companies   businessmen

and _____ problems as our problems, and of
    businesswomen

their _____ future as our future. Whether you are
      industries

_____ Auto Service or _____ _____ Clothes
Moe   Rodriguez   Women

Store or _____ or _____ University, our firm will
         Macy   Rutgers

commit _____ resources to helping you, as we have done for
       it

_____, _____, and _____.
General Motors,   Sears,   other

Answer is given on the next page.

Answer

When a company's *profit margin starts to dwindle, or when the profit margin of one of its* subsidiaries *does, then it's time to call on one of the business* world's *multitude of consulting firms. Let us recommend* ours. *We have an accounting staff* whose *training amounts to over 125 years of service, and* theirs *is a quality hard to equal. Our* experts' *duty is to spend all their time and effort solving the problems of the* country's *leading* companies. *We think of these* businessmen's *and* businesswomen's *problems as our problems, and of their* industries' *future as our future. Whether you are* Moe's Auto Service *or* Rodriguez' Women's *Clothes Store or* Macy's *or* Rutgers University, *our firm will commit its resources to helping you, as we have done for* General Motors, Sears, *and* others.

COMMAS

Commas are used to separate one part of a sentence from another part of a sentence.

Commas do not always go with, or always not go with, any particular word. The perennial questions (Do you use a comma after *however?* after *therefore?* before *and?*) show a screaming ignorance about what commas are for. Commas can appear before or after any word in the language, if the sentence structure requires. They do not attach to words, but *separate one part of a sentence from another part*.

English has only four and a half occasions when you should use commas. When you don't know whether to use a comma, simply hold up these rules and see if any one of them applies:

Rule 1. Use a comma with *and, but, or, for, nor, so, yet* to separate two complete sentences.

Rule 2. Use a comma to separate a long introduction from the rest of the sentence.

Rule 3. Use commas to separate items in a series.

Rule 4. Use commas—one before and one after—to separate an interrupter from the rest of the sentence.

Rule 4½. Use a comma to separate elements that could be misunderstood if read together.

Here goes.

Rule 1. Use a Comma with *and, but, or, for, nor, so, yet* to Separate Two Complete Sentences

Ask two questions: (1) Do I have two complete sentences? and (2) Do I have *and, but, or, for, nor, so, yet*? If (and only if) both answers are yes, use a comma.

Thus:

	Two Complete Sentences?	And, but, or, for, nor, so, yet?
1. The president entered the room, and he brought his three assistants with him.	Yes	Yes
2. The president entered the room and brought his three assistants with him.	No	Yes

See? If the subject isn't repeated, you have only one sentence and therefore no comma. Try two more on your own:

	Two Complete Sentences?	And, but, or, for, nor, so, yet?
3. The firefighter smashed open the elevator and the frightened passengers stumbled out.		
4. The firefighters smashed open the elevator and let the frightened passengers stumble out.		

Answers: Comma in number 3 but not in number 4.

Now take a look at two particularly troublesome examples:

	Two Complete Sentences?	And, but, or, for, nor, so, yet?
1. Sales in our phosphate division have been declining steadily; therefore we have decided to let phosphate go and instead concentrate on other areas.	Yes	No

In this example, the absence of *and, but, or, for, nor, so, yet* means you can't use a comma, but clearly something has to be there. The semicolon, as shown, is one answer; another possibility would, of course, be a period and capital letter. Still another would be to say "and therefore" instead of just "therefore" (comma required, because now you have an *and*), and still yet another would be simply to substitute "so" for "therefore" (again with a comma, since *so* is one of those seven words).

	Two Complete Sentences?	And, but, or, for, nor, so, yet?
6. The president announced his resignation; however we all knew he had been fired.	Yes	No

Just as with sentence 5, you have to punctuate, but you can't use a comma because there's no *and, but, or, for, nor, so, yet*. Either use a semicolon (as shown) or change "however" to "but."

Therefore and *however* are the language's two most troublesome words with respect to Rule 1. They are not in the *and, but, or, for, nor, so, yet* list and therefore cannot be used with only a comma to separate two complete sentences. With them you must use stronger punctuation—a semicolon or a period—to accomplish the separation.

This is not just an arbitrary rule; it makes entirely good sense. Very quickly, here's the explanation. *However* and *therefore* can occur either at the beginning or at the end of a phrase, so you've got to signal to your reader which way you want the word to be read. Look at these examples:

You do not have top security clearance, however.

However, if you need access to the files we will make other arrangements.

Okay, those are clear. But now look at what happens if the sentence says this:

You do not have top security clearance, however, if you need access to the files we will make other arrangements.

See? Here, you can't tell whether the "however" goes with the first half or the second half of the sentence. You must provide a complete stop on one side or the other of the "however"; otherwise, the reader will have to go back and reread.

Quick final question: Are these two sentences correct?

1. We do not believe, therefore, that any serious wrongdoing has occurred.

2. You should not believe, however, that this episode will be forgotten.

Answer: Sure. Since each example consists of just one sentence, not two, Rule 1 doesn't apply at all.

So when somebody asks if you can have a comma both before and after *however* or *therefore*, the answer is "Look, bubble-gum-brain, commas don't go with words—commas *separate one part of a sentence from another part of a sentence.* Commas can appear before or after absolutely any word in the language, if the sentence structure requires."

Rule 2. Use a Comma to Separate a Long Introduction from the Rest of the Sentence

If you have two parts of a sentence, and the first part is long but isn't a complete sentence in itself, then put a comma after the first part to separate it from the rest of the sentence.

Examples

Having been with the company since the early years of the Depression, he felt he was entitled to a larger pension.	[Long introduction]
On Tuesday he will be 70 years old.	["On Tuesday" isn't long.]

Warning: Don't let a long subject phrase trick you into thinking it's an introduction:

The reason he decided to leave us after all these years was that he couldn't stand the cigarette smoke.	[It's not an introduction at all: "The reason was."]

Rule 3. Use Commas to Separate Items in a Series

This is the easiest rule of the bunch. Almost nobody ever makes mistakes with this one.

Examples

The growth areas are insurance, real estate, and health care.
It is a labor-troubled, debt-ridden, mismanaged company.
IBM, Xerox, General Motors, and Eastman Kodak are recruiting here
    next month.
Our president is in Chicago, our treasurer is in Los Angeles, and our
    board chairman is in Paris.

Note: Editorial usage permits you to leave out the comma after the next-to-last item in a series, the one before the *and*. That one, some people say, doesn't need more separation, because the *and* is already there. Nonetheless it's better to put it in: "X, Y, and Z" is always clear, but in some instances "X, Y and Z" isn't. Look at this sentence, for example: "This semester I am taking Marketing, Calculus and Finance and Economics." Is it "Calculus and Finance" or "Finance and Economics"? Without a comma, there's no way to tell.

Rule 4. Use Commas—One Before and One After— to Separate an Interrupter from the Rest of the Sentence

If your sentence contains some little phrase that interrupts the normal flow of things, like this, you should separate that interrupter from the rest of the sentence by putting commas both before and after. Note—two—one before and one after. It's usually better to have no commas at all than to have just one.

You were notified, I understand, about the inspector's arrival.
Use LIFO, not FIFO, to maximize your profit in times like these.

Please believe me, dear readers, when I say this bores me as much as it does you. I first met you in Warren, Ohio, on July 8, 2007, a Tuesday, I believe.

Sometimes *who* and *which* phrases are interrupters, and sometimes they're not. To tell, apply this test: if the phrase is needed to *identify* the person or thing *for the first time*, then it's not an interrupter, so you don't use a comma. But if it is *not* needed to identify the person or thing for the first time, then it *is* an interrupter, and you do need commas before and after it.

Examples

The Charles Wilson who works in the stockroom is here to see you.

[The *who* phrase is needed to tell you which Charles Wilson it is. Obviously there's more than one "Charles Wilson," or the writer wouldn't have said "The." Thus it's *not* an interupter—no commas.]

Charles Wilson, who has worked with the company 36 years, plans to retire in June.

[This *who* phrase *isn't* needed—it tells you something about Mr. W. but doesn't serve to "identify" him; thus it *is* an interrupter, and therefore commas are required.]

Company picnics, which are well attended, occur in June.

[The *which* phrase describes something about the picnics, but it doesn't "identify" them. Thus it *is* an interrupter—commas required.

Company picnics which occur in June have the best attendance.

[This *which* phrase *does* identify which picnics you're talking about— the ones that are held in June—and thus it's *not* an interrupter—no commas]

Don't worry about all this. Rule 4 is mostly just common sense. If something interrupts a sentence, like this phrase, put commas around it—both sides.

Rule 4½. Use a Comma to Separate Elements That Could Be Misunderstood If Read Together

Sometimes you need to use a comma even though none of the first four rules applies, because, if you don't, your reader might read together some words that don't belong together.

Here are examples. Each requires a comma:

Inside the people were running around.

["Inside" certainly isn't a long enough introduction to qualify under Rule 2, but if you omit the comma, your reader will surely read "Inside the people"—as you just did—and then have to go back and start the sentence again.]

Since he tried to escape his punishment was increased.

[Again, don't let your reader be lured into misreading it as "tried to escape his punishment."]

After washing up the boss's wife, Joe, and I came to dinner.

["After washing up" is short, but if you omit the comma, your career will be too.]

And finally, consider these:

Before leaving the company
officials, the inspectors
gave one last warning.

Before leaving the company,
officials met with the employees.

Before leaving, the company
officials met with the mayor.

Before, leaving the company
officials used to require 20
minutes of handshakes.

[See? Commas
are signals to
tell your
reader how you
want your sentence
to be read.]

SEMICOLONS AND COLONS

The semicolon and the colon serve altogether different functions. Nobody should ever have cause to confuse them.

The Semicolon

The semicolon is just like the period in a couple of ways—that is, it makes the reader come to a complete stop, and it has to have complete sentences both before and after it. But it has one huge difference: instead of just "stop," it means "stop but don't go away till you've read the next part too." In other words, when the grammar calls for a total stop, but the thought calls for continuity, then you use a semicolon.

Examples—in which the writer wants to be sure that the reader doesn't stop before getting to the end of the sentence:

The stock could be bought on margin; I certainly do not recommend doing such a thing, however.

Rice and sherbet are on the boss's diet; potatoes and ice cream are not.

Use of the semicolon is almost always grammatically "correct" as long as both the part before it and the part after it form complete sentences that could stand by themselves. If they don't form complete sentences, the semicolon can't be used. Test it by substituting a period; if you can do so, it's used correctly.

As for being used *appropriately*, that's a more subjective matter. The best way of testing it is to see if what follows the semicolon in some way *elaborates on what went before*. If it does, the use of the semicolon is appropriate.

The Colon

The colon, like the period and the semicolon, makes the reader come to a complete stop, but it differs in other ways. It doesn't have to have a complete sentence after it, and it doesn't mean just "stop."

It is a bugle blast that signals that an announcement is about to take place. It says "Look, everybody, at what comes next: THIS!" What follows the colon thus can be just about anything—a sentence, a phrase, a word, a list, a scribble—but whatever it is it always in some way *restates what went before*.

Examples

The company's directors gave three reasons: prestige, growth, and diversification.

The president read slowly through the list of donors: Aaron, Abeston, Acker, Addison, and so on.

My priorities are ordered as follows: completing my book, undertaking the consulting project, and submitting designs for the new office building.

There's only one word to describe her work: phenomenal!

Be sure you understand the different signals these two marks send to the reader. The semicolon indicates elaboration, the colon restatement:

Elaboration	Restatement
There's optimism today; stock prices are sharply higher.	There's good news today: stock prices are sharply higher.

One more note on the colon: since the colon makes the reader come to a complete stop, it should not be used in a place where stopping would be awkward. Look how much more readable the sentence on the right is:

Awkward

Our company's overseas
problems are: financial,
cultural, and motivational.

More Readable

Our company's overseas
problems are financial,
cultural, and motivational.

Finally, spacing: two after a colon; one after a semicolon.

[two after a colon]   [one after a semicolon]

DASHES AND HYPHENS

Dashes and hyphens have the misfortune to look a little bit alike—a misfortune (that was a dash) because they have absolutely no connection with each other, being entirely different-feathered (that was a hyphen) birds.

The Dash

A dash indicates a complete stop in a sentence—see? It can take the place of a semicolon, a colon, or even—in fact—commas or parentheses. The way it differs from those other marks is by being more abrupt and therefore dramatic—a sudden breaking off, for effect.

Some writers—especially young ones—romantic flair and all that—tend to use the dash often—very, very often. It does create a catchy rhythm that keeps the reader hopping, and it can be very effective in some kinds of writing. But in business writing, where the style should stay as unobtrusive as possible and not divert attention from the subject, dashes shouldn't be used much.

The Hyphen

A hyphen is used just the opposite way from the dash. Instead of separating things, it hooks them tightly together, so that nobody can misread them as individual words. You must never permit anybody to think you have said "Our employees work in a well" when what you really said was "Our employees work in a well-designed factory." "Half yearly raises" could be taken to mean just 50 percent of a normal year's raise; if what you mean is every six months, you must say "half-yearly." "Less organized crime" probably means less crime; if instead you mean they haven't got it together, you have to say "less-organized." See? Nobody can ever misunderstand if you say "well-designed," "half-yearly," and "less-organized," all with hyphens; without them, misunderstanding is possible.

Rules for hyphens are pretty sloppy and unhelpful, but these three hold true most of the time:

Rule 1. **If there's a chance of misreading, and a hyphen can prevent it, use a hyphen.** A sentence that starts off "She is an animal" can be read with a meaning different from one that starts off "She is an animal-lover." Don't wait for a rule to tell you to put a hyphen there; do it simply to prevent confusion.

Rule 2. **Hyphenated phrases are far more likely to be needed before a noun than after.** "He is a well-qualified candidate," but "The candidate is well qualified"; "Our company has heavily-used computers," but "Our company has computers that are heavily used." The reason is the same as before: you don't want your reader to think you've said "He is a well," so you have to say "well-qualified"; yet when you say "The candidate is well qualified," no such confusion exists, so you don't have to use a hyphen. "Our company has heavily used computers" might sound like a statement about something our company has often done, so you have to say "heavily-used"; but with "Our company has computers that are heavily used," there's no ambiguity and thus no need for a hyphen.

Rule 3. **If you have an *-ly* word, you are less likely to need a hyphen.** "He is a poorly qualified candidate" and "She is an unjustly maligned administrator" are incapable of being misread, so no hyphen is required, even though the phrases occur before the noun. "A much-abused privilege" has a hyphen; "a widely abused privilege" usually doesn't.

Spacing?

A **Hyphen** has no spaces around it, thus-like.

A **Dash** consists of two hyphens, with no spaces around them--like thus.

Your computer will probably turn the two hyphens into one long dash. That's okay—let it do so.

SPELLING

Of the mechanical errors that occur in writing English, misspelling accounts for more than half. Do not, therefore, hurl your cookies because you've found a section here on spelling. If you have spelling problems, read these pages.

Remember that the spelling-check device on your computer won't help you if the misspelled word you write happens to be a correct word, as in *then/than*, *principal/principle*, and *effect/affect*.

English spelling is a bit of a mess, mostly because the language wasn't designed by anybody but instead just sort of haphazardly accumulated its words and sounds from many places and over many centuries. The resulting anomalies are so numerous that no simple rules can begin to take them all into account.

What does make the problem more or less manageable, however, is that the same errors keep occurring again and again. Practically all of them derive from the imperfect correlation of spelling and sound, an unfortunate fact of life that English writers have to live with. Learning to handle the following six problems (listed starting with the worst) will prevent about 95 percent of all the usual misspellings.

Problem 1. Doubled or Not-Doubled Letters

Early in a Word

The rules for doubling or not doubling a consonant early in a word aren't helpful. Just look carefully at the following 27 words and try to figure out some rules of your own, or at least some way of remembering the spellings:

accelerate	accommodate
access	accumulate
accessory	across

address   interrupt
affidavit   misspell
aggregate   necessary
aggressive   occasion
amendment   occurred
amount   omission
appropriate   professional
around   recommend
exaggerate   success
excellent   unnecessary
imagination

Here are a few possible rules you might have noticed:

- If *c*'s are pronounced as *k*'s, then there must be two *c*'s, not just one: *access, eccentric, occidental*.

- If, however, *c*'s are pronounced as just *s* instead of *k*, then there's probably just one *c*: *acetic, acidic, necessity*.

- If the accent is on the preceding vowel, chances are good that the consonant that follows is doubled: *aggravate, allocate, appetite*. But *amendment* and *imagination* don't double their consonants, because the accent comes later in the word. Note one big exception: *aggressive* and *aggression* do double their *g*'s, even though the accent comes afterward.

- If the opening syllable is one of those standard prefixes like *dis-* or *mis-* or *un-* or *re-*, just add the rest of the word without changing anything: *disservice, disappoint, misspent, misspell, mistaken, unneeded, unopened, recollect, recommend, recompense*.

- If you still can't tell whether a letter is doubled or not, try fiddling around with other forms of the word. Thus you might not remember whether *professor* has one *f* or two, but you might be able to recognize that *profess* has just one, and then you would know. You might not know at firsr whether *business* has one *s* at the beginning or two, but you would certainly know that *busy* has just one, and then you'd know. Or the number of *m*'s in *omission* might puzzle you, but if you think of *omit*, then you'll know it's just one.

- If, after all this, you still can't decide whether or not to double a letter early in a word, look it up, a step that probably would have saved you time to start with.

Later in a Word

Rules for doubling, or not doubling, consonants at the ends of words are much better. Very simply, you double a consonant if and only if both of the following conditions are met:

1. It's in the accented syllable.
2. Doubling is needed to preserve the pronunciation.

Thus *admitted* and *emitted* and *omitted* double their consonants, but *vomited* doesn't (syllable isn't accented). *Referring* does, but *offering* doesn't (same reason). *Planning* does (because both rules apply), but *complaining* doesn't (no effect on pronunciation). *Gassing* does. *Occurred* and *occurring* do. *Bussing* ought to, but the big bus companies don't agree.

Note that if you had to drop an *e* before adding a suffix, then you don't double the consonant: come coming, dine dining, cure curing.

By the way, these rules about doubling letters later in a word don't apply to British English. The British double practically everything.

Problem 2. Frequently Confused Words

No rules apply here. Read through this list and see if you find any that have ever given you trouble.

accept—take, agree to (acceptance)
except—but, omit (exception)

adapt—change something so it fits your needs
adopt—accept something completely, without change

advertise (That's an *s*, not a *z*.)

adv**ic**e (a noun)—what an adviser gives: "a word of advice"
adv**is**e (a verb)—what an adviser does: "Please advise me."

all ready—totally prepared, or everybody prepared: "We are all ready to go."
already—by this time: "The contract is already signed."
all right (two words)

a lot (two words, two words, two words!)

affect (a verb)—to influence: "It affected my thinking."
effect (a noun)—an influence: "It had an effect on us."
effect (a verb, and less common)—to bring about: "The mayor tried to
    effect three reforms during her term."

although (one word)
even though (two words)

am**o**ng
am**ou**nt

arti**cle**

attained—got there: "The company attained its goal for the year."
obtained—came into possession of: "We have obtained a season pass."

attribute (a verb)—give credit or blame for: "He attributes his success to his
    mother."

contribute—donate: "She contributes to the college every year."

boundary
foundry

capitol—the building
capital—All other meanings are spelled this way.

choose, chose, chosen

cite—refer to
site—location
sight—vision

complement—fit together
compliment—praise, without charge

conscience—moral sense
conscious—aware
conscientious—hard-working, sincerely believing

course—procedure
coarse—rough

council—group, committee
counsel—advice, lawyer

criterion (singular)
criteria (plural)

disinterested—impartial, not taking sides
uninterested—bored with the whole thing

do to—take action on something
due to—as a result of

draught—drink
drought—dry spell

dual—two parts
duel—contest

e.g.—for example
i.e.—that is to say

elicit—coax out of: "He tried to elicit an opinion from the
    presiding officer."
illicit—illegal, against the law

emigration—leaving
immigration—coming in

eminent—prominent
imminent—about to happen

ex**c**itement
exercise

fair—good-looking, played according to the rules,
    or a carnival
fare—prosper ("The company is faring well"), food, or
    what you pay the bus driver

fami**lia**r
similar

foregoing—what went before
forgoing—voluntarily doing without: "I will forgo my vacation
this year."

formally—officially, properly
formerly—once upon a time

fourth—between third and fifth
forth—onward

height, weight
length, strength

higher—taller
hire—employ

incidence—frequency
incidents—happenings

in spite of (three words)
despite (one word)

its—belonging to it
it's—it is, or it has

lead (a noun) (pronounced *led*)—element Pb, or the stuff in
your pencil
lead (a verb) (pronounced *leed*)—to conduct. *Mislead* means to
lead somebody in the wrong direction today.
led (a verb)—conducted. *Misled* means to have led somebody in
the wrong direction yesterday.

lose, lost, lost (verbs)
loss (a noun)
loose (an adjective)

manufacture (as a verb)—to make something
manufacture (as a noun)—the thing that's made
manufacturer—the company that makes the thing

moral—right, or the lesson at the end of a fable
morale—spirit within a company

peak—top
peek—get a secret glance at
pique—arouse

perspective—outlook: "You have a good perspective on the issue."
prospective—possible in the future: "She is a prospective employee."

persuade
peruse
pursue

principal—(1) chief, (2) head of a high school, or (3) money that gathers interest
principle—rule

predominant—occurring more than any other
prominent—important

quiet—not making noise
quite—very

reign—rule
rein—harness

respectfully—showing respect
respectively—in this same order

sched**ule**

stationery—writing paper; what the station**er** sells
stationary—not moving

surprise (Notice the first **r**; also, that's an **s**, not a **z**.)

than—compared to
then—at that time, or as a result

their—belonging to them
there—not here
they're—they are

to—(all other meanings not included in the next two)
too—more than enough; also "also"
two—between one and three

us**ed** to

wary—cautious
weary—tired

weather—rain, sun, snow, and so on
whether—choice of two or more things

your—belonging to you
you're—you are

Problem 3. The *Uh* Problem

English has quite a large number of unpronounced vowels—in words like *grammar* (pronounced *gram-uhr*) and *vulgar* (pronounced *vul-guhr*), *comparative* (*compar-uh-tive*), and *competition* (*comp-uh-tition*). As far as the sound goes, the *uh* could be just about any letter at all.

To see if you can figure out what letter it actually is—and use of the wrong letter is a very common problem—try fiddling around with others forms of the word to see if, somewhere, the *uh* has a sound. Thus you might try these:

Uh Word	Other Form	Therefore, Correct Spelling Is
approx(UH)mate	prox**im**ity	approx**i**mate
ben(UH)fit	be**nef**icence	ben**ef**it
comp(UH)tition	comp**et**e, comp**et**itive	comp**et**ition
compet(UH)tive	comp**et**ition	comp**et**itive
defin(UH)te	defi**nit**ion	defin**it**e
d(UH)vide	di**vv**y	di**v**ide
differ(UH)nt	differ**ent**ial	differ**en**t
dim(UH)nution	di**min**ish	dim**in**ution
exist(UH)nce	exis**ten**tial	exist**en**ce
experi(UH)nce	experi**ent**ial	experi**en**ce
gramm(UH)r	gramm**at**ical	gramm**a**r
med(UH)cine	me**dic**inal	med**i**cine
permiss(UH)ble	permiss**iv**e	permiss**i**ble
prefer(UH)nce	prefe**ren**tial	prefer**en**ce
prep(UH)ration	pre**par**e, pre**par**atory	prep**ar**ation
rep(UH)tition	rep**et**itive	rep**et**ition
r(UH)diculous	**rid**icule	r**id**iculous
sim(UH)lar	si**mil**itude	sim**il**ar

But for other words you simply have to learn them, especially the *-ant/-ent* and *-ance/-ence* ones. Here are some of the worst troublemakers:

apparent	intelligent
appearance	irresistible
ascendant	minuscule
comparative	obstacle
dependent	occurrence
descendant	opportunity
describe, description	perseverance
despair	persistent
desperate	pleasant
despite	predominant
destroy, destruction	prominent
eliminate	sacrifice
grievance	sacrilegious (from *sacrilege*,
hangar (at the airport)	not from *religious*)
independent	separate
indispensable	superintendent

Problem 4. The Silent-Letter Problem

Some words contain letters that aren't pronounced anymore, sometimes never were. Here are the most common troublesome silent-letter words:

acknowledge	conscious
acquaint	debt
acquire	different
acquisition	discipline
boundary	environment
business	excellent
conscience	excitement

exhaust

exhilarate

fascinate

fifth

gauge

government

guard

quantity

recognize

surprise

temperament

temperature

twelfth

valuable

Problem 5. The Suffix Problem

Lots of words, especially those ending in *-y*, cause grief when various endings are added to them. Here are some prominent nuisances among the *-y* words:

Root Word	+s	+ed	+ing	+er
Words That End in *-ay*				
lay	lays	laid	laying	layer
pay	pays	paid	paying	payer
say	says	said	saying	sayer
Words That End in Consonant + *-y*				
baby	babies	babied	babying	babier
bury	buries	buried	burying	burier
carry	carries	carried	carrying	carrier
muddy	muddies	muddied	muddying	muddier
study	studies	studied	studying	studier
Words That End in Consonant + *-ey*				
jockey	jockeys	jockeyed	jockeying	jockeyer
money	monies	moneyed	—	—
monkey	monkeys	monkeyed	monkeying	monkeyer
valley	valleys	—	—	—

Root Word	+s	+ed	+ing	+er
Words That End in *-ie* or *-ye*				
lie (recline)	lies	lay	lying	lier
lie (fib)	lies	lied	lying	liar
die	dies	died	dying	dier
dye	dyes	dyed	dyeing	dyer

Problem 6. *-ie* and *-ei*

Three rules govern most *-ie* and *-ei* words:

Rule 1. The usual order is *-ie*: bel**ie**ve, gr**ie**ve; **lie**ge, s**ie**ge; bel**ie**f, ch**ie**f, gr**ie**f, rel**ie**f.

Rule 2. Following a *c*, however, the order is reversed: conc**ei**t, dec**ei**ve, rec**ei**pt, rec**ei**ve.

Rule 3. Also, if the word rhymes with *day*, use *-ei*: **ei**ght, inv**ei**gh, n**ei**ghborhood, w**ei**ght.

A few exceptions occur. Notable among them is *seize*.

GRAPHS AND CHARTS

The four questions about graphs are (1) whether, (2) where, (3) how, and (4) which.

Whether to Use a Graph

Yes, yes, yes. Use as many as you sensibly can. Well-drawn graphs are tremendous attention grabbers and are more effective than many pages of prose in making a point. Look at any issue of *Bloomberg Businessweek* to see how graphs can make a smashing headline for an article. You'll find things like this:

Figure 1

Wiftandia's Balance of Payments Is Improving Dramatically

(billions of US $)

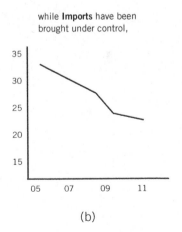
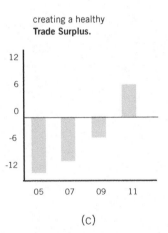

Having seen only this much (12 square inches, 30 seconds) you already have a clear outline of the whole subject.

Where to Put the Graphs

First of all, a graph should come *after* the discussion in the text. Tell us what to look for, and then when we get to the picture, we'll be ready for it. As for the physical location of graphs, put them as close as you can to the text they illustrate, right on the same page if possible. If that can't be done, make certain the text refers the reader to the chart number at exactly the crucial place. Charts exist to help the reader see the point, and the further they get from the place where that point is explained, the less good they do.

How to Draw Graphs

Four basic principles apply to all kinds of graphs. Pay attention. If graph-constructers followed these, the quality of the world's graphs would soar.

Principle1. Dominant Impression

A graph is supposed to show something, to make a subject clearer than if no graph existed. That sounds pretty obvious, but an alarming number of graphs simply don't clearly show anything at all. You have to study and restudy them before you can finally figure out their point.

To avoid subjecting your reader to such a trial, always be sure your graphs have a *dominant impression*—a clear rising or falling, or the converging or diverging or parallelism of two lines, or the equal or unequal market shares held by various companies, or the correlation or noncorrelation of two trends, and so on. In other words, a mere topic isn't enough: a graph must have a thesis, and it must make a point. And the point must be visually obvious at first glance.

For example, a well-drawn graph will have as its purpose not to show "how Cherry Hill spends its taxes" but to show that "Cherry Hill spends almost twice as much on schools as on government"; not to show "car sales over the past decade" but to show that "small cars have made great gains in market share in 10 years." See the difference? It's the famous difference between a thesis and a mere topic. Graphs must have a thesis.

If no thesis, no dominant impression, is clearly evident, then nothing has been gained by drawing a graph in the first place. A graph that looks like a plate of spaghetti is a bad graph. Since it doesn't depict any trend or make any point, it might as well have been left as a bunch of numbers in a table.

Principle 2. Titles and Labels

Always give your graph a title, so that the readers instantly know what they're looking at and what its point is. The title should tell the thesis: not "Gold Prices" but "The Rise in Gold Prices Resumes"; not "SAT Scores" but "The Decline in SAT Scores Is Coming to an End." This way the point of the graph will leap out at the reader.

The same is true of every line, every axis, and every bar and scale and color in your graph. Don't let yourself get so wrapped up in graph drawing that you forget to tell your reader what everything means. To say it again, the graph exists to make things clearer. If the graph itself becomes a puzzle that has to be explained, it's a bad graph.

Principle 3. Customary Uses of the *x* and *y* Axes

By general agreement the *x* axis is usually reserved for time or for the number of items, and the *y* axis for money or for percent. For instance, in Figure 2, which shows the rise in the price of oil during the 1970s, the *x* axis represents years, and the *y* axis represents price.

Figure 2

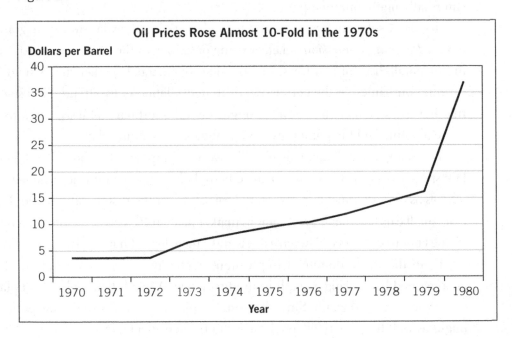

For another example look at Figure 3, which shows comparative success rates of a fund-raising campaign over several months. Again the x axis represents time, but here the y axis represents percent.

Figure 3

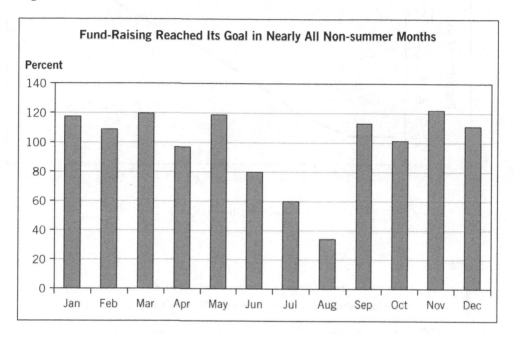

An *item count*, such as population size (Figure 4) or number of pianos sold (Figure 5) can occupy either the x or the y axis with equal appropriateness, depending on what it's being plotted against.

Figure 4

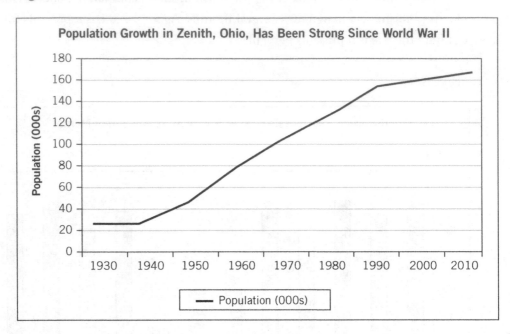

Figure 5

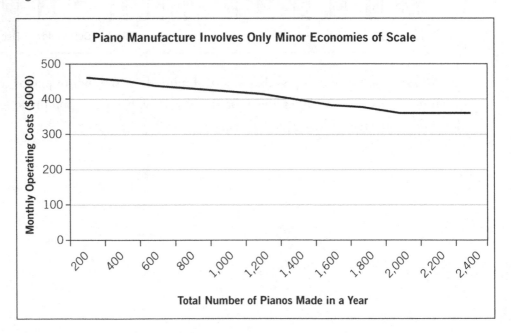

Principle 4. Limited Numbers of Variables

The simplest graphs plot two variables against each other. A third variable can usually be added without losing clarity, and sometimes even a fourth is possible. Fifth variables have been known too, but then you're starting to get into never-never land, drawing Rubik's graphics. Don't forget that the purpose is to make a point clearer by illustrating it; when the graph itself becomes a challenge to the reader, you've lost sight of your purpose.

Look, for instance, at the question of increasing complexity. Figure 6 is a simple two-variable graph showing (1) the number of workers in (2) various professions.

Figure 6

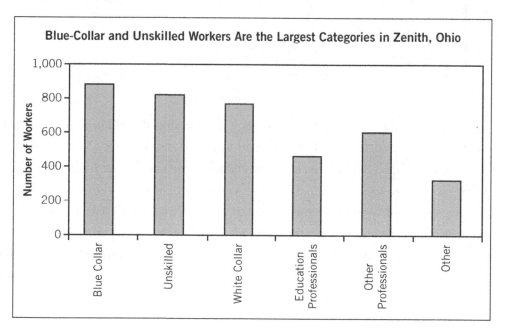

If you add *time* to it—showing how the numbers have changed over the years—then you have three variables as shown in Figure 7.

Figure 7

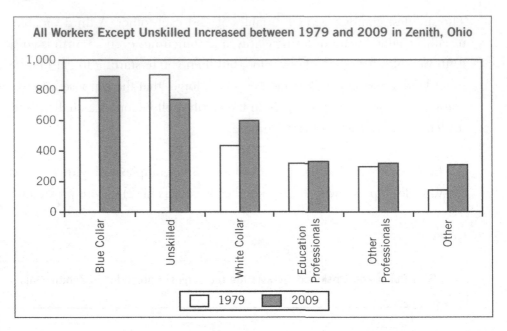

All Workers Except Unskilled Increased between 1979 and 2009 in Zenith, Ohio

Legend: 1979, 2009

Categories: Blue Collar, Unskilled, White Collar, Education Professionals, Other Professionals, Other

Mathematically speaking, you don't have to stop there. How about the number of *men* and the number of *women* in each category in 1979 and 2009? And why not *black men* and *black women* and *white men* and *white women*? And while we're at it, how many 20- to 45-year-olds and 45- to 70-year-olds in each group who are registered *Democrats* and registered *Republicans*? And *Christian, Jewish,* and *Muslim*? *Vegetarians* and *carnivores*?

Although mathematically possible, such complications would take a graph far beyond the boundaries of good sense. Just remember that you are trying to show something, not to create a repository of data.

Which Kind of Graphs to Draw

Graphs come in unlimited varieties, but (1) line, (2) bar, (3) pie, and (4) fishtank are the most important.

Line

A line graph (Figures 1(a), 1(b), 2, 4, and 5) illustrates a *trend*. It shows what happens to one variable as time passes or as expenditures increase or as population grows or as the quantity of manufactured goods goes up. *You must have continuous scales on both axes*: you cannot draw a trend line connecting plumbers with truck drivers, or New Jersey with Idaho, because such a line has no significance between the labeled points. But you *can*, of course, connect 50 with 100, because the points in between represent everything from 51 to 99.

Bar

A bar graph (Figures 1(c), 3, 5, 6, and 7), unlike a line graph, does permit comparison of discrete entities, like plumbers and truck drivers, or New Jersey and Idaho. One of the scales still must be continuous, but the one with the bars on it doesn't have to be. Bars can, moreover, be subdivided for still further usefulness—male and female truck drivers, 1910 and 2010, Republican and Democrat, and so on. The bar graph is very versatile and very easy to read.

Pie

A pie graph (Figure 8) can be used only when you have a finite total—when you know what 100 percent is. It is extremely easy to read, because it instantly shows how big a portion of the pie goes to each item. But it also is very confining, since it has really only this one use. It cannot show time or changes, and it cannot compare things that aren't part of the same group. It would, for example, be useless if you wanted to show projections of month-by-month auto sales at General Motors during 2008, or how steel imports compared to steel exports.

Correctly used, the pie chart makes its point better than any other kind of chart could do. Look how this one makes its point immediately and unmistakably clear. Anybody can see in an instant the size of each portion and how the portions relate to one another.

Figure 8

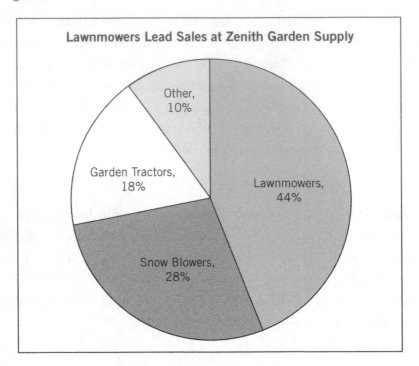

Lawnmowers Lead Sales at Zenith Garden Supply

Other, 10%

Garden Tractors, 18%

Lawnmowers, 44%

Snow Blowers, 28%

Fishtank

Also called an area chart, a fishtank graph (Figure 9) is like a combination line and bar graph, in that it permits both a comparison of several trends and a comparison of quantities at any one point in time. Or, to be even more confusing, it's like a pie graph that is dragged through time so that it shows how the slice sizes change. From Figure 9 you can instantly see the increase in gas and oil use over the past century and the simultaneous decrease in coal use, and yet you can also see how they compared in any one year: coal provided more than half the nation's energy in 1920 and gas only about 12 percent, but in 1975 coal provided only about 9 percent while gas provided more than 33 percent. The chart also permits a great sweeping view: from it one can instantly see that, overall, during the past 65 years coal has provided a little less than half our energy, and gas and oil a little more than half.

Figure 9

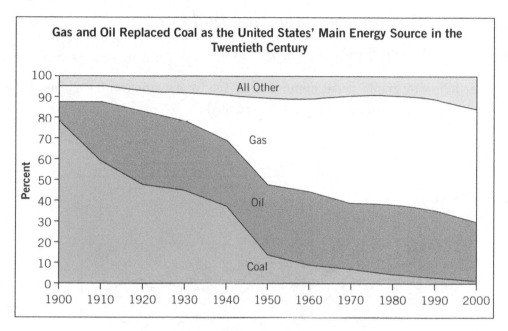

Gas and Oil Replaced Coal as the United States' Main Energy Source in the Twentieth Century

Practice: Improving Bad Graphs

Each of the following graphs needs improvement. Tell what's wrong with each and how the subjects could have been more appropriately presented.

Bad Graph 1

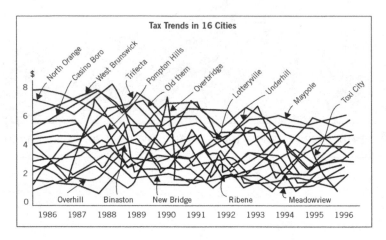

Bad Graph 2

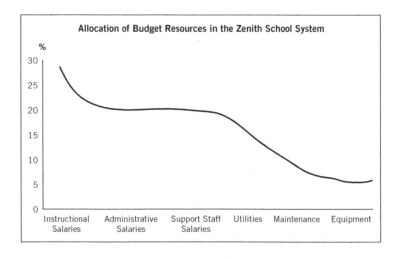

Bad Graph 3

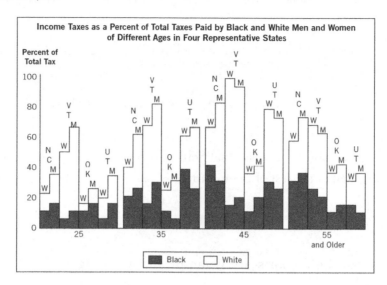

Income Taxes as a Percent of Total Taxes Paid by Black and White Men and Women
of Different Ages in Four Representative States

Practice: Designing Good Graphs

Sketch out appropriate graphs to show the following variables.

1. How many employees were present at Schlerg's East Orange plant each day during last summer?

2. How do Schlerg's three plants compare in overall attendance rates?

3. What was Schlerg's sales revenue during each of the last 27 years?

4. What are Schlerg's various debts—to whom and how much?

5. What percentage of Schlerg's employees are black, white, Hispanic, or other?

6. Historically, what percentage of Schlerg's employees were black, white, Hispanic, or other in each of the last 27 years?

7. How does Schlerg compare in sales with the 10 other leading household products companies?

8. What is the amount of Schlerg's sales in each of the seven geographical regions of the United States?

9. How do Schlerg's sales for this year compare with those for last year in each of the seven regions?

10. How does the increase or decrease that Schlerg experienced in each region this year compare with that of the rest of the industry?

The answers are given on the next pages.

Answers

1. *Since the x axis here is continuous, you could use a line graph. You could equally well use a bar graph, with skinny bars representing each of the summer days. In either case you will have a challenge coming up with a dominant impression and thesis-like title. Depending on what you find, the point of the graph might be "Attendance Dropped on Mondays and Fridays during the Summer," or "Attendance Was Lower in August Than in July," or maybe just "Attendance during the Summer Hovered around 75 percent."*

2. *Here you have to use a simple bar graph with three bars representing the three plants. The y axis will have to show percentage, in order to take into account the different sizes of the plants.*

3. *A line graph is the obvious choice here, but 27 bars would also do. The title, reflecting the dominant impression, would say something like "Sales Revenues Have Risen Only Slightly in 27 Years" or "Revenues at Schlerg Have Fluctuated over the Years."*

4. *Since the total debt is knowable, a pie chart is the obvious choice. It would pictorially show the percentage owed to each debtor, and the labels on each slice could show the actual amount. You could, of course, use a bar graph with a bar for each debtor (arranged from largest to smallest, or the other way around). That would show the amounts clearly, but the percentages would be harder to see.*

5. *Either a bar or a pie will do here. Since the question is "percentage" rather than number, the pie is probably better. If the question had asked for the number in each group, then the bar would offer more advantages.*

6. *Here, the fishtank is the obvious choice, because you're showing changes in percentages over time. The x axis would show the 27 years, and the y axis would range from 0 to 100 percent. Each stratum could be shown in a different color, to make it instantly clear which group has been growing fastest and which slowest, relative to the others. If the question had asked for actual numbers rather than percentages, then you'd probably be better off with a line graph featuring four lines.*

7. A bar chart is the only possible choice here. Since you have figures for only 11 companies rather than the entire industry, a pie chart would be wrong, and since there's no time component you can't use lines. You will have 11 bars, one for each of the companies, arranged from largest to smallest or smallest to largest, in order to give a visual impression, and maybe you can highlight the Schlerg bar by giving it a color. The title might say "Schlerg Ranks Third in Sales among the Top 11 Companies."

8. Either a pie or bar chart will do here. Either kind can show both the amount and the comparison among the regions. The title will say something like "Midwest Accounts for the Largest Part of Schlerg's Sales."

9. This one almost has to be a bar graph, with two side-by-side bars for each region. You could, of course, use two pie charts next to each other, but it's much harder for a reader to compare the differences between two pies than between two bars. The title will need to call attention to what the comparisons show — like "Sales Have Risen in the Southern and Western Divisions."

10. This one isn't as much of a problem as it might appear at first. A bar graph is the only possibility. You can simply use two side-by-side bars for each region. You need to make clear which bars represent Schlerg and which the industry, and you need to make the title call attention to whatever the overall point is — something like "Schlerg Is Doing Better Than the Industry in Six of the Seven Regions."

If you were to try to draw a graph that has still more variables than these — for instance separating sales for both Schlerg and the industry into "household products," "garden products," and "automotive products" — then you start to go over the cliff. The graph becomes a messy repository of data instead of a clear illustration of a point.

A NOTE ON *A*, *AN*, AND *THE*, FOR NON-NATIVE SPEAKERS OF ENGLISH

Speakers of other languages, especially Asian languages, often have trouble trying to figure out when to use *a*, *an*, and *the* in English. No wonder. Even native speakers who can intuitively tell whether a *the* is needed find it hard to explain what the reason is. To complicate the situation even further, British usage and American usage are widely different, as in "He is in hospital" (British) but "He is in the hospital" (American).

Generally—and this is very generally, with lots of exceptions—the following rules apply.

Rule1. If It's Singular and Countable, Use *a*, *an*, or *the*

Countable

> The dog runs around the corner and into the street.
> [One dog, one corner, one street]

> The organization is governed by a committee.
> [One organization, one committee]

Not Countable

> Steel and aluminum are important in construction.
> [Steel, aluminum, construction—all not countable]

Cooperation is important in establishing good spirit in a company.
[Cooperation and spirit aren't countable; "company," however, *is* countable.]

Rule 2. If It's Plural, You Usually Don't Use *the*

Use *the* only for *specific things you've already mentioned before:*

Not Specific

Dogs are running loose.
[This means just "some dogs"—you don't know which ones or who they belong to.]

Corporations that avoid taxes will get in trouble.
[This means "corporations in general" and "taxes in general"—it's true about all corporations and all taxes.]

Specific

The dogs are running loose.
[This means that your reader knows which specific dogs you're referring to.]

The corporations pay taxes.
[This means certain specific corporations that you've already been referring to—your reader understands which ones. And since it says "taxes" rather than "the taxes," it means "all taxes," not just certain specific ones.]

Corporations pay the taxes.
[This means that all corporations pay the certain specific taxes that you've been referring to.]

Part III

RESEARCH TECHNIQUES

MYTHS AND REALITIES

Research is one of the most misunderstood kinds of writing. Everybody has written research reports, and nearly everybody has done them wrong. Here are some common myths and realities:

Myth	Reality
Research writing consists of finding documentation for what you're going to say.	Research is a discovery. You don't know what you're going to say until you've done the research.
Research consists of finding an answer.	Research consists of finding evidence—facts and ideas. Then you study the evidence and arrive at your own answer.
Research consists of changing the words of your sources.	Even if you change somebody else's words, the ideas are still somebody else's. Your job is not simply to report what somebody else said but to make up your own mind after considering all the things other people have said.
A research report is a report with footnotes.	Footnotes don't make something research. If you put footnotes on a piece of garbage it's still garbage.

Myth

The Internet has made research really easy, because you can find a million sources in just a few seconds.

Reality

Evaluating a million sources is a hundred thousand times harder than evaluating ten. Sure, it's easier to *find* sources, but research consists of *using* them, and that involves your brain, not your computer. Research, even in the computer age, continues to be the most difficult and most time-consuming of all kinds of writing.

The quality of research writing has declined markedly in the past 50 years, both in student work and in published articles and books. The central reason (along with the pressures resulting from the frantic pace of our lives) is that researchers have allowed the photocopier and the Internet to substitute for their brains. Research consists of three phases: we *find* information, we *process* it in our brains, and we *disseminate* the results. No question about it—the *finding* and the *disseminating* have been made a lot easier by technology. But that second phase—the *processing*—hasn't, and it never will be. It still involves fundamental brainwork that requires time, patience, and judgment.

THE NINE STEPS IN RESEARCH

Research of all kinds consists, inevitably, of these nine steps:

Area
Topic
Tentative source list
Working source list
Notes
Thesis
Skeleton plan
Final plan
Writing

Step 1. Area

The **area** is the general field you're scouring around in to find a topic you can research. If you're interested in corporate social responsibility (CSR), then that's your area. Likewise, if you're interested in Adam Smith or Thomas Edison, then those are your areas. The economy of Finland is an area. They're not the subjects you're writing about; they're merely areas in which you're going to find something to write about.

Step 2. Topic

The **topic** is the question you decide to find an answer to. "Does a high level of CSR produce high enough stock price increases to justify its cost?" is a topic. "What were Adam Smith's religious views, and how did they affect his thinking in

The Wealth of Nations?" is a topic. "How was Thomas Edison's research laboratory organized and managed?" is a topic. "To what extent is Finland's economy independent of those of the other Scandinavian countries?" is a topic.

In each instance, it's a specific question you're going to try to come up with an answer to. You are not, not, not writing about "CSR in general," or "just a report about who Adam Smith was," or "Thomas Edison's lab," or "a description of Finland's economy." Those things are only areas; now you're identifying something you want to find out within one of those areas. This difference between an *area* and a *topic* is huge, basic, and central, and it's essential for you to understand. People who don't understand the difference can never write a satisfactory research report. Think of research as a *quest,* as a *search,* as setting out on a *mission* to come back with an answer to a specific question. If you don't know precisely what you're looking for, you won't find it.

Step 3. Tentative Source List

The **tentative source list** is just what it says—a list of all the places where you think you might find useful information about your topic. For instance, you figure that some books, articles, and encyclopedias might tell you what Adam Smith's religious views were, so you jot down a few references that you think, just from the titles, might be useful. But before you jot, get organized: you'll need to know where you found these references, where they're located, and, later on, whether you've looked at them or not and whether you found them useful. So you might as well plan ahead. Using the form on the next page will ensure that you have written down everything you'll need. It's on a separate page here so that you can reproduce it and use it.

Source	Citation	Location	Seen?	Action
1				
2				
3				
4				
5				
6				
7				
8				

So here is what the form would look like after Step 3:

Source	Citation	Location	Seen?	Action
Library catalog 1	Adam Smith, *The Wealth of Nations* (1776)	Univ. Library HB161 .S65		
Amazon 2	Pike Royston, *Adam Smith, Founder of the Science of Economics* (1966)	Public Library Y330.1 Sm51p		
Library catalog 3	Siegmund Feilbogen, *Smith* . . . (sometime before 1923)	Univ. Library HB103		
Library online periodical index 4	Eric Schliesser, "Reading Smith after Darwin," *Journal of Economic Behavior & Organization* 77 (Jan. 2011), 14-22	Online		
" 5	Margaret Schabas, "Adam Smith's Debts to Nature," *History of Political Economy* 35 (2003 supplement), 262-281	Online		
" 6	Robert B. Ekelund, "Adam Smith on Religion and Market Structure," *History of Political Economy* 37 (winter 2005), 647-660	Online		
" 7	Charles G. Leathers, "Adam Smith on Religion and Market Structure: The Search for Consistency," *History of Political Economy* 40 (summer 2008), 345-363	Online		
" 8	Thomas J. Ward, "Adam Smith's Views on Religion and Social Justice," *International Journal on World Peace* 21 (June 2004), 43-62.	Online		

Source	Citation	Location	Seen?	Action
Library online periodical index 1	Feridun Yilmaz, "Adam Smith: A Moral Philosopher and His Political Economy," *Journal of Economic Issues* 44 (Dec. 2010), 1108-1109	Can't find		
Google 2	"Adam Smith" in Wikipedia	Online		
Footnote in #2 3	R. H. Coase, "Adam Smith's View of Man," *Journal of Law and Economics*, 19 (Oct. 1976), 529-546	Online		
Library online periodical index 4	Lisa Hill, "The Hidden Theology of Adam Smith," *European Journal of the History of Economic Thought* (spring 2001), 1-29	Online		
" 5	James Lavey, "The Hidden Theology of Adam Smith: A Belated Reply to Hill," *European Journal of the History of Economic Thought* 11 (Dec. 2004), 623-628	Online		
" 6	Lisa Hill, "Further Reflections on the 'Hidden Theology' of Adam Smith," *European Journal of the History of Economic Thought* 11 (Dec. 2004), 629-635.	Online		
Google 7	"Adam Smith," in *The Concise Encyclopedia of Economics*	Online		
8				

Step 4. Working Source List

The **working source list** is what you arrive at after you've perused the items that you listed in the previous step. These are what's left after you've identified the ones you can and can't use. You haven't actually read them yet, but you've scanned them carefully enough to decide whether or not they're usable. In perusing the previous list, you've been able to find all but one of the 15 items, and you've decided to use only seven of the 14 you've found—rejecting the others for various reasons (like not being directly relevant, or for being in a foreign language, or for being too long to read in the time available, or for having been written for children). Thus the last two columns of the form can now be completed. It looks like this:

Source	Citation	Location	Seen?	Action
Library catalog **1**	Adam Smith, *The Wealth of Nations* (1776)	Univ. Library HB161.S65	Y	No—too long to read
Amazon **2**	Pike Royston, *Adam Smith, Founder of the Science of Economics* (1966)	Public Library Y330.1 Sm51p	Y	No—a children's book
Library catalog **3**	Siegmund Feilbogen, *Smith . . .* (sometime before 1923)	Univ. Library HB103	Y	No—in German
Library online periodical index **4**	Eric Schliesser, "Reading Smith after Darwin," *Journal of Economic Behavior & Organization* 77 (Jan. 2011), 14-22	Online	Y	No—not relevant to religion
" **5**	Margaret Schabas, "Adam Smith's Debts to Nature," *History of Political Economy* 35 (2003 supplement), 262-281	Online	Y	No—not relevant to religion
" **6**	Robert B. Ekelund, "Adam Smith on Religion and Market Structure," *History of Political Economy* 37 (winter 2005), 647-660	Online	Y	Yes—debate with 7
" **7**	Charles G. Leathers, "Adam Smith on Religion and Market Structure: The Search for Consistency," *History of Political Economy* 40 (summer 2008), 345-363	Online	Y	Yes—debate with 6
" **8**	Thomas J. Ward, "Adam Smith's Views on Religion and Social Justice," *International Journal on World Peace* 21 (June 2004), 43-62.	Online	Y	Yes—very useful

Source	Citation	Location	Seen?	Action
Library online periodical index 1	Feridun Yilmaz, "Adam Smith: A Moral Philosopher and His Political Economy," *Journal of Economic Issues* 44 (Dec. 2010), 1108-1109	Can't find	N	Skip—only 2 pages long anyway
Google 2	"Adam Smith" in Wikipedia	Online	Y	No—too general—did get one ref.
Footnote in #2 3	R. H. Coase, "Adam Smith's View of Man," *Journal of Law and Economics,* 19 (Oct. 1976), 529-546	Online	Y	Yes—very useful
Library online periodical index 4	Lisa Hill, "The Hidden Theology of Adam Smith," *European Journal of the History of Economic Thought* (spring 2001), 1-29	Online	Y	Yes—debate with 5 and 6
" 5	James Lavey, "The Hidden Theology of Adam Smith: A Belated Reply to Hill," *European Journal of the History of Economic Thought* 11 (Dec. 2004), 623-628	Online	Y	Yes—debate with 4 and 6
" 6	Lisa Hill, "Further Reflections on the 'Hidden Theology' of Adam Smith," *European Journal of the History of Economic Thought* 11 (Dec. 2004), 629-635.	Online	Y	Yes—debate with 4 and 5
Google 7	"Adam Smith," in *The Concise Encyclopedia of Economics*	Online	Y	No—doesn't mention religion
8				

Step 5. Notes

The **notes** are often, in fact just about always, considered the most important step in research. This is where you actually *read* the items in your working source list—not photocopy them, not copy and paste them, but read them. This is where the information you've found gets transformed into the thing you're going to produce. It takes a long time, and it absolutely must not be rushed. You must read, carefully, all the way through each of your sources, making sure you understand the author's main point, and meticulously writing down any fact that you think might be useful later. You also need to keep careful records of page numbers.

Whether you write your notes on cards or on worksheets, you've got to write them out. You can even write them on your computer, if you can find some way to make the computer split the screen so you can read from one page while you're writing on another. This is the central moment in the research. You're not underlining, selecting from, or pasting in text from your sources: you're taking the ideas and transforming them into something that pertains to the question you're trying to answer.

Here's an example of how a source might be transformed into notes.

This Is What the Source Said

How are tsunami waves different from normal ocean waves? Both normal ocean waves and tsunami waves can be described by their period (time between two waves), wavelength (horizontal distance between waves), amplitude (wave height), and speed. Normal ocean waves are caused by the wind, weather, tides, and currents. They have periods of 5 to 20 seconds, wavelengths of 100 to 200 meters (300 to 600 feet), and travel at speeds of 8 to 100 kilometers per hour (5 to 60 miles per hour). Tsunami waves have much longer periods of 10 minutes to 2 hours, wavelengths of 100 to 500 kilometers (60 to 300 miles), and travel at speeds of 800 to 1000 kilometers per hour (500 to 600 miles per hour). The amplitudes of normal waves and tsunami waves are similar in deep ocean water, but near shore, tsunami waves can be much larger with heights of 10 meters (32 feet) or more. Furthermore, normal ocean waves only involve motion of the uppermost layer of the water, but tsunami waves involve movement of the entire water column from surface to seafloor. This means a normal wave is like a small ripple on top of the ocean, but tsunamis are like the entire ocean getting deeper all at once.

Source:
NOAA's National Weather Service
Pacific Tsunami Warning Center
http://ptwc.weather.gov/ptwc/faq.php

This Is What the Notes Might Look Like

Note card 27

NOAA's National Weather Service
Pacific Tsunami Warning Center
http://ptwc.weather.gov/ptwc/faq.php
Accessed 3/23/12

Tsunami waves differ from regular waves in five ways:

1. **Further apart in** *time* **(10 minutes to 2 hours, compared with 5 to 20 seconds)**
2. **Further apart in** *distance* **(60 to 300 miles, compared with 300 to 600 feet)**
3. *Higher* **(32 feet or more, when close to the shore—no figure given for regular waves)**
4. *Much faster* **(500 to 600 mph, compared with 5 to 60 mph)**
5. *Layer of water involved* **(tsunami waves go all the way to the bottom of the ocean, while regular waves involve just the topmost layer)**

Remember above all, your job is to evaluate, not just to accept. You're not merely passing on to your reader what you've found. Some of the things you find will be reliable and some won't, and your job is to distinguish between them and to use the reliable and disregard the unreliable.

When you finish this step, you should have a pile of notes—not just one or two cards or worksheets, but a whole pile.

Step 6. Thesis

The **thesis** is what you decide to say after reviewing your notes. Study the notes over and over, and then some more, taking notes on your notes, indexing the ideas, until you are absolutely sure you know what you want to say. The thesis is the answer to the question you were asking back in Step 2. Once you have decided on your thesis, you're more than halfway through the whole project, even though you haven't yet written a single word of the final report.

Step 7. Skeleton Plan

The **skeleton plan** refers to the order in which you decide to present your thesis. Since you know what you're going to say, the logical next thing to decide is what you're going to say first, second, third, and so on.

Step 8. Final Plan

The **final plan** correlates the notes from Step 5 with the order you've decided on in Step 7—what pieces of evidence from your notes you're going to present in support of each of your points in your skeleton plan. If, for example, the third point you're going to make about Adam Smith's religion is that he broke from ancestral tradition in some of his beliefs, then you need to identify those parts of the notes that tell what his ancestors' beliefs were and those parts that tell how he differed from them. So you simply note under point 3 that you will use evidence from, for example, "note cards 9, 14, and 17."

Step 9. Writing

The **writing** is all that's left, and it's pretty much on automatic pilot. Since you know what you're going to say in what order, even down to the level of knowing which pieces of evidence you're going to present in support of each point, you have very few decisions left to make. Just follow the rules from the first part of this book, and you're in.

FIVE OTHER SUGGESTIONS ABOUT EFFECTIVE AND EFFICIENT RESEARCH

Here are some additional suggestions in the following five areas of the research phase:

Variety of sources
Availability of information
Minimal photocopying and printing
Being organized
Writing

Variety of Sources

It's not just that you need to have several sources—you need to have several *different kinds* of sources.

One reason is that every kind has its limits. Books are marvelous storehouses of ideas that probably will never make it to the Internet, but the data they contain is inevitably older than what you'd find in current periodicals and on the Internet. Periodical articles are much more current, but they're very uneven in quality and reliability. And the Internet itself—ah, the Internet! Remember that although the Internet appears to be an almost limitless storehouse of information, the only reason anything appears on the Internet is that somebody put it there on purpose. You've got be wary of what that purpose is—an advertisement, a political statement, a desire to boost (or damage) somebody's or some company's reputation, an encouragement to invest in something, and so on. Just as books, ages ago, were considered to be practically infallible—for centuries people said "It is written!"—so today the Internet has the same mystique, and maybe worse. Compensate for the weaknesses of each kind of source—books, magazines, the Internet—by making use of the other kinds too.

A second reason is that the different kinds of sources provide different kinds of information. A search engine is great for last quarter's earnings figures but not for whether a company is a nice place to work. Investigative reporting that appears in magazines and newspapers will tell about things like dubious working conditions and the machinations of insider trading—as well as about any really successful and innovative management arrangements that a company might have adopted. And books will present ideas that are too intricate to be summed up in a few pages. Each kind of source supplements the others.

Availability of Information

Don't underestimate what you can find out. Far more information is available in a business library, and online, than most people realize. Furthermore a lot of it is free. You can find almost anything either in books, on the Internet, or in library-subscription online services. If you're stumped, find a business reference librarian and ask for help. The librarians are amazingly knowledgeable.

Minimal Photocopying and Printing

Keep photocopying to a minimum. People sometimes seem to confuse copying with reading: as soon as they find a magazine article, they press the print button or rush to the copy machine. Then $2 and 10 minutes later, they look at the copy to see if it's relevant. That's dumb. Instead, when you find something possibly relevant to your subject, just sit down and look it over for five minutes. If it's useful, then take notes on it. Use photocopying and printing only for hard-to-copy charts and tables that you'll need to refer to often.

Being Organized

Go about your work in an organized way! You can waste the rest of your life doing research if you don't put some structure into your activities. Get all your citations together before you examine any of them in detail. If you have to look at each volume of a 20-volume set, write out the numbers from 1 to 20 and tick them off as you see each volume. Keep a log of what you've consulted. Make notes to yourself about what each article you looked at said, even if it didn't say anything useful. That way you won't have to wonder tomorrow if it's something you should look at again.

Writing

And finally, when you start to write, don't forget that research reports have to be organized and written just like any other kind of report, with a what-and-what-order thesis paragraph, directionally-pointed subheadings, and classically structured paragraphs.

GENERAL TIPS ABOUT DIFFERENT KINDS OF RESEARCH

It would be pointless, counterproductive, and misleading to provide a list of specific reference sources here. New ones keep coming out every month, and old ones keep disappearing every time there's a technological innovation or a budget cut. What can be useful, however, is a discussion about each of five different kinds of research: (1) ideas and terms, (2) people, (3) companies, (4) products or industries, and (5) countries.

Ideas and Terms

If you want to know about *zero-based budgeting*, *Pareto's Law*, *management by objectives*, *market segmentation*, *arbitrage*, *swap defaults*, *gap analysis*, or any other such phrases that keep popping up in business talk, you're in luck. You have a choice of several fine published dictionaries that specialize in business—for instance *The McGraw-Hill Dictionary of Modern Economics*, which contains brilliant one- and two-paragraph explanations of about 1,400 phrases. Another source is the whole series of dictionaries (management, investing, computers, international trade, marketing, banking, and more) by Jerry M. Rosenberg. Or if you want to do it online, you can go to The Glossarist (www.glossarist.com), Business Dictionary (www.businessdictionary.com), or a few others.

People

By all means, do consult the standard reference works like *Who's Who in America* and *Who's Who in Finance and Industry*. But (1) don't believe everything they say! Those reference books contain biographical sketches written by the person himself or herself, the who's who-ee. Even if they don't contain outright lies as they sometimes do, they're certain to be highly selective and include only the kinds of information the person wants you to know. Nobody would ever, for example, put in something like "Sing Sing Prison, 2008-2011." And (2) be sure that you don't stop with just these sources: you absolutely must also consult the really important information, the subjective things found in magazines and newspapers. There you will find articles in which an investigative reporter has dug into matters such as what the person is like to work with and how coworkers feel about the person's abilities—subjects that will never show up in reference works or websites. When you're researching a person, this kind of information is at least as important as objective facts.

Companies

Facts are important when you're researching a company, but again, it's important that you don't rely only on factual and statistical sources. And don't pay any attention *at all* to the company's own website, which is nothing but an advertisement. Is the company well managed, innovative, charitable, environmental, and decent to its employees? You'll never find that kind of information in statistical tables, and what the company's website says is, of course, totally unreliable. Go to periodical sources—newspapers and magazines—to find out subjective information. Several wonderful online business periodical indexes exist that not only identify articles but even give you the full text.

However, when you do need statistical and factual information—and you obviously do when you're researching companies—you have some really good places to go to. In addition to some fine sources like *Value Line* and Mergent, you have the government to help you. Every publicly traded company has to file "disclosure" information with the Department of Commerce, and the information includes even things like details about pending lawsuits. You can find out a lot of very reliable factual information, in fact practically anything, about companies.

Products or Industries

For this kind of research you will need three different kinds of information. One is **statistical**—increasing or decreasing production, raw material costs, and such things. Second is **news about developments in the industry**—technological, regulatory, health hazard, import/export, and so on. Third, you will need to know about the **competitors**—who they are, how big they are, where they're located, and how much market share they have. The first and third kinds you can find in reference and statistical sources, but for the second kind you will need to rely mostly on newspapers and magazines.

Basic to nearly all your research about products and industries is an understanding of the NAICS numbers—North American Industrial Classification System—which replaced the SIC (Standard Industrial Classification) system a decade ago. NAICS is a numerical index of all businesses, and so many reference tools use it as their way of organizing information that you have to know how to use it. An important thing to understand is that NAICS numbers are to be thought of as decimals. Thus 3 is larger than 29, which is larger than 265, which is larger than 2589, which is larger than 24906, which is larger than 239886. And as the number gets more digits, what it refers to becomes more specific. For instance:

31	includes	manufacturing of all food and textiles
311		manufacturing of all food
3115		manufacturing of dairy products
31151		manufacturing of non-frozen dairy products
311511		manufacturing of milk
311512		manufacturing of butter
311513		manufacturing of cheese
31152		manufacturing of frozen dairy products

The Commerce Department's "Census of Manufactures" (online) will get you started. From there, rely on the reference guides available on university library websites—for instance http://libguides.rutgers.edu.

Countries

In just the last few years a whole bunch of printed and online reference tools have sprung up with vast amounts of information about individual countries and world trade. You can find out practically anything.

Concerning **countries**, you can find detailed information about the economy, demographics, political situation, labor force characteristics, business activity, productivity, business regulations, tax and tariff policies, and imports and exports. Concerning **world trade**, plentiful statistics are available about production, consumption, foreign direct investment, imports and exports, and much more.For both country information and trade information, you can use the free and continually updated online guides on many university sites—for example http://libguides.rutgers.edu/countries and http://libguides.rutgers.edu/trade_stats.

FOOTNOTES

All right, all right. Even though footnoting is not what research is all about, it's true that footnotes do frequently turn up in research. So here's a discussion. The three questions everybody asks about footnoting are (1) whether to, (2) when to, and (3) how to.

Whether to Footnote

Here, as in every other decision you have to make in business report writing, the sole criterion is *understandability*: will footnotes make the reader more likely to understand your point? If the report is only a memo to your supervisor, and the question you're answering is a simple factual one where the reliability of your sources isn't an issue, the answer is **no**. Footnotes would be unnecessary and just get in the way.

But suppose the report, although still just a memo to your boss, does contain some very startling information that will affect an upcoming decision. Then your boss will definitely, and quite correctly, insist on knowing where you found your facts. So somewhere in the memo report you must identify the source. Otherwise you won't be persuading anybody.

This is, after all, a pretty basic point. If somebody runs into your office shouting "IBM has just declared bankruptcy!," you will certainly ask "How do you know?" How you react will depend on the answer. "It's in today's *Wall Street Journal*" will produce one response, but "My neighbor's four-year-old daughter told me" will produce a different one. Clearly, you have to identify your source.

Actually, you have three reasons for providing documentation: so that your reader will know (1) how much faith to put in your findings, (2) where to go to check them out, and (3) where to go to read more about the subject. Documentation is thus a very important element in a research report. Your purpose is to convince your readers of the point you're making, and if you don't show them what your sources are then you won't convince anybody of anything.

But that still doesn't answer the question of whether the documentation should be in the form of a footnote, or in a note at the end of the report, or in the text itself. Ask yourself whether more is gained by making your reader look at the bottom of the page[1] or by putting a note at the end that says, "Source: *Journal of Marketing Research*, April 2009, p. 236"; or by including the source information in the body of the report itself—for example, "You will be interested to know that the *Journal of Marketing Research* for April 2009 says that . . ." Chances are good that, if the report is just a memo, you'll choose one of the last two options: memos rarely have footnotes because their contents are sufficiently uncomplicated for a simple allusion to the source to do the job.

Not so, however, with longer reports. Here you will be making not one but several points that need attributing to a source, and just about the only way to do it clearly and with precision is through footnotes.

So to the time-honored question, "Geez, do you wannus to use footnotes?," the answer, as always, is that circumstances determine whether you should or shouldn't. If it can make any difference to your reader what the source of your information is, then you must find some way to identify the source. And whether you choose to use a footnote or an appendix or just a phrase in the report itself is determined by—guess what—understandability.

---

[1] Like this.

Practice: Choosing the Best Kind of Documentation

Tell what kind of footnote or other note would be appropriate in each of the following situations.

1. Your boss asks you to check the Yellow Pages to see if your company has a listing in each place where your competitors are listed, and to write him a report about what you find.

2. Your boss asks you for a report on the probable amount of increase in heating costs for the next two years.

3. Your boss asks you for an explanation of the phrase *gross private domestic investment*.

4. You discover that employee benefits at six other companies are lower than at your company, and you write your boss a report showing the difference.

Answers are given on the next page.

When to Footnote

People often think that footnotes are required only for direct quotations, but oh not so, not so, not so! Once you have determined that your report is the kind that requires footnotes, then you must use them not just for (1) word-for-word *quotations* in quotation marks but also for (2) *paraphrases* in which you have taken the idea from a source but expressed it in your own words, as well as for (3) any *idea* that has been remotely suggested to you by a printed source, and even for (4) any *fact* that can't be considered common knowledge. Failure to footnote under any of these circumstances can get you in a pile of trouble.

Okay—we pause for a moment to answer a frequently asked and very reasonable question: "Since I didn't know *anything at all* about this subject before I started researching, then absolutely everything in my paper has to have been taken from a source! Doesn't that mean I have to footnote practically every word?"

The answer is no, and the explanation lies in the rules about paragraph structure, discussed above on pages 27 to 40. Remember say-it, explain-it, detail-it, and say-it-again? In the process of doing research, you first gather some information. Then you study it to see what it all means. Then you write a say-it sentence stating the point, or conclusion, you have arrived at from studying this information.

That's your own conclusion, something you reached all by yourself, so it doesn't require a footnote.

Then you decide how to present the information. You settle on presenting Fact A and then Fact B and then Fact C, in that order. So you write an explain-it sentence, telling how you're going to set up the rest of the paragraph. That's your own decision, something you decided all by yourself, so it doesn't require a footnote.

Now you get around to presenting the evidence that has led you to decide what you've decided—Fact A and Fact B and Fact C. Aha! These are things you found somewhere, things you wouldn't have thought of if you hadn't read the sources, things that aren't common knowledge, so this time you **do** need to footnote them.

And finally, now that you've said it and explained it and detailed it, you are going to drive your point home by saying it again and showing how all the parts fit together. This is, again, entirely your own work, your conclusion from examining the evidence, so it doesn't require a footnote.

Got it?

Say it	No footnote
Explain it	No footnote
Detail it	Yes, footnotes
Say it again	No footnote

If it would help to have an example, try this one:

It is not surprising that the MBA began to enjoy a much-enhanced reputation at mid-century, as people and the universities themselves began to think of it as a servant of society rather than just a shortcut to making lots of money. The new attitude was evident both in statements and in practice. In an address at a University of North Carolina

Say it: no documentation required

Explain it: no documentation required

dedication in 1953, Harvard's Dean David said *Detail 1* that business schools had increased their usefulness and expanded their purpose and thus had gained wider acceptance. Their mission, he concluded, was no longer simply seen as teaching young men and women how to run a business but was now recognized as "providing creative leadership for business, labor, and government."* His view was confirmed in practice *Detail 2* when other schools recognized the virtues of the education business schools were providing and began to emulate them. Some engineering schools, for example, such as the one at UCLA, added business courses in the mid-1950s for the purpose of training engineers to become executives.* The *Say it again: no docu-* formerly scorned MBA had now acquired a halo. *mentation required*

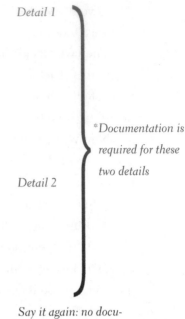

Documentation is required for these two details

Remember, anyhow, the purpose of footnotes: not merely (1) to give credit, but (2) to enable your readers to judge how reliable the information is, and also (3) to let them know where to look if they want to read still more on the subject.

Now: Consistent with these four occasions for footnotes and these three reasons for footnotes, you should follow this one rule: footnote as seldom as possible. Too[2] many[3] footnotes,[4] especially ones that occur at an inappropriate[5] place in the middle[6] of a sentence,[7] interrupt the progress of a report so seriously that they badly interfere with understandability. Footnotes are there to help the reader; if they make the reader's task harder, they're being used incorrectly.

---

[2]Or even very.

[3]The exact definitions of *many*, *too many*, and *very many* are left up to the individual reader.

[4]The term *footnotes* is used here to include all notes, whether or not they literally are located at the foot of the page.

[5]Such as between an adjective and the noun it modifies.

[6]Or at the end.

[7]Similar observations may be found in other style manuals also. For example, see the *MLA Handbook for Writers of Research Papers* or the *Chicago Manual of Style*.

How to Footnote

Four major systems of footnoting exist, a situation that used to cause great anxiety but no longer has to. Their names are *Chicago*, MLA, APA, and ACS, and they all have different ways of doing things. With *Chicago* you use a number, and the reader has to go look at the numbered note. With MLA you put the author's name and the page number in parentheses right in the text itself. With APA you put the author's name and the date of the book in parentheses in the text. And with ACS you have a numbered list of citations at the end, and you put the relevant number or numbers in the text.

But you don't have to know all this anymore, or even what the footnote looks like, because some computer angels have come to your rescue. You can buy software that does it for you (EndNote is one, ProCite is another), or you can find help online at Purdue University's Online Writing Laboratory (OWL) (http://owl.english.purdue.edu) or at Firefox's Zotero site (http://www.zotero.org). Most of the time you can just tell the computer which footnote system you want to use and then plug in the information, and, poof, you've got your footnote.

Part IV

OTHER THINGS

LETTERS AND E-MAIL

Business letters have to be organized and efficient, just as business reports have to be. But letters are different in enough ways to require a separate set of rules. Here are five.

Rule 1. Write as if You Were Speaking

Do not use weird phrases like "In reference to the above-captioned communication," "Please be advised that we are in receipt of," "We beg to acknowledge your esteemed favor of the nineteenth," or "Per your request, herewith enclosed is." Nobody talks that way, and nobody should write that way. Letters are by nature personal, so they should sound personal.

Rule 2. Identify the Purpose of the Letter as Close as Possible to the First Sentence

Since letters never have a title and usually don't even have a subject line, the reader has to begin reading without any advance warning of what the letter is all about. Thus you've got to announce the point pretty quickly. Don't risk irritating—and losing—your reader by starting off with irrelevant pleasantries about the weather. Nothing is really gained by starting off with introductory idle chatter, even if it's a letter containing bad news. Just get to the point.

Here are some good opening sentences:

I am interested in the assistant controller position advertised in Sunday's *Star-Ledger*.

This is a letter of complaint concerning one of your drivers.

Would someone from your firm be available next month to speak to a senior citizens' group about investing?

> We are deeply concerned about the problems you raise in your letter of
> June 23.
>
> With deep regret, I must notify you that we have decided to eliminate
> your position with the company.

Note that this rule does not require that a "thesis statement" appear at the first or that the order of the rest of the letter be spelled out here. All it requires is that the first sentence, or pretty close anyhow, should tell the reader what the letter is all about—that is, why you're writing it.

Rule 3. Don't Give Any Information You Don't Have To

Do not be so foolish as to say "Our company is very interested in the possibility of acquiring a controlling interest in your firm, and I would like to have lunch with you next Thursday to discuss the idea." Instead say "Could we have lunch together next Thursday?" Do not be so foolish as to say "Your employment with our company will be terminated, effective July 1, because of frequent tardiness, a large number of customer complaints, and poor programming abilities." Instead say "Your employment with our company will be terminated, effective July 1."

The reason for not saying too much, of course, is to keep you out of trouble. If you send that first letter, tomorrow's *Wall Street Journal* will proclaim "Schlerg Considering New Acquisition: Spokesperson Says Company 'Very Interested.'" If you send the fully explained letter to the programmer, you will have committed your company to a long and tedious process of proving tardiness, documenting the customer complaints, and testing the employee's programming skills. If you had just shut up in time, neither of those things would have happened.

Rule 4. Do Give All the Information You Have To

If you're scheduling an appointment or a meeting, tell the time, date, place, room number, and purpose. If stating a price, say "$89.95 plus $14.50 shipping and handling, for a total of $104.45"—not just "plus shipping and handling"—since the purchaser has to know the full cost. If payment by check is involved, tell who the check should be made payable to. Omitted information is a too-common and altogether inexcusable problem in business letters. Before you write the letter, make a list of facts the recipient could possibly need, and then, after you've written the letter, go back and be sure they're all there.

Rule 5. Be Absolutely Clear about What Response You Expect, or What Steps Are to Be Taken, and When, and by Whom

A letter expressing "concern" or one complaining about a malfunction in your car but not saying what you expect to be done about the problem, is a wasted letter. Let your reader know, very precisely, what you want as a result of writing your letter, and whether or not you expect a reply, and by when.

One further note about letters: no agreement seems to exist now about what greeting to use in a letter—especially a feminine or unisex equivalent of "Dear Sirs" and "Gentlemen." Here are some entirely acceptable possibilities:

Dear IBM:
Dear Vice President:
Dear Customer Service Department:
Ladies/Gentlemen:
Gentlemen/Ladies:

If you are writing to a unisex name like "Pat Orkney" or "Chris Stopher" and you don't know whether it's a man or a woman, you can simply write "Dear Pat Orkney" or "Dear Chris Stopher."

One other option: you can just omit a greeting altogether.

All those rules apply to e-mail too. Here are five more that apply to e-mail specifically:

Rule 6. In E-mail, Have a Subject Line, and Be Sure It Says Something Specific

A subject line that says only "Hi," "A Question," or "Interesting Fact" is of almost no use, and it's of no use at all when the recipient wants to go back later and figure out which e-mail it was that included certain information. Be sure that your subject line is specific enough to make that particular message distinguishable from all the others you've sent.

Rule 7. Plan before You Start Writing

Stop and think about the tone you'd like to use, the purpose of the message, the details you need to include, the specific question you're asking. **Then** you can start writing.

Rule 8. Proofread!!

Proofread the e-mail address, the subject line, and the message—word by word, letter by letter—especially the last-minute changes you made. Do it at least three times. More than half the e-mail messages that people send contain typographical errors that would never have slipped by in a letter.

Rule 9. Be Specific about Dates

Don't say just "today" or "tomorrow," as you would in conversation. Your reader probably can't tell what day you mean.

Rule 10. Pause before You Send

Just look everything over one more time. Are you sure this is what you want to send? Are you sure you're sending it only to the person you want to send it to and not to everybody on a list? Are you sure you attached what you said you were going to attach? Are you sure the address is correct, right down to the periods and @s, and the subject line too? Is this the best way you can convey the information or ask the question? When you're finally sure, and only then, click on "send." Remember, those e-mails that begin "Please ignore my previous e-mail" are really irritating, because the reader has already read the previous e-mail before getting to the "ignore" message.

Practice: Examples of Good and Bad Letters

The following two letters are bad. Identify all the problems with each of them.

Bad Letter 1

SCHLERG CORPORATION
248 UNESCO Avenue
East Arlington, New Jersey 07000

November 30, 20—

Mr. Robert Z. Purple
3932 Legation Street
Chevy Chase, Maryland 20039

We are in receipt of yours of the 25th, and in reply please be advised that the Order Department has been apprised of your complaint as regards stock item #368-24-D.

We are therefrom notified that the aforesaid item is currently unavailable and will be backordered pursuant to your request.

Please be assured of our full cooperation in this matter. If we may be of further assistance, do not hesitate to contact the undersigned, who remains,

Yours truly,

Elmer V. Schlerg
Vice President

123 Escalon Plaza
Sueville, Oregon 88869
November 23, 20—

Mr. Osbert K. Schlerg, President
The Schlerg Corporation
2498 Beale Boulevard
Saidville, Oregon 82498

Dear Mr. Schlerg:

I was born in this county 59 years ago and have always lived here. My wife, whom I married thirty-eight years ago, also was born here. We have always been good citizens of this county and have never thought about moving.

When I came to work for your father forty years ago, I was at first a mailboy. After two years I was moved onto the production line, where I remained for a long time before taking my present position four or five years ago. I have always enjoyed working for your company and have made many friends here.

It was a major surprise to me to hear that I am being let go. Everybody I have talked to also was quite surprised.

I look forward to hearing from you.

Sincerely,

John J. Johns

The following letter is a good example.

Good Letter

4789 Smithall Street
Newark, New Jersey 07102
December 12, 20—

Mr. Peter N. DeWolf
ABC Industries
9876 Broad Street
Newark, New Jersey 07103

Dear Mr. DeWolf:

I am very interested in the junior financial analyst position you are currently advertising for and would appreciate your examining my credentials to see if you think I might be qualified.

As the enclosed résumé indicates, I am completing my MBA at Weymarsh University, with emphasis on finance and international business, and have held related full-time and part-time positions in two companies in New Jersey.

My interests are in all kinds of financial analysis, especially in matters involving foreign trade. Eventually I would like to direct an international marketing campaign. I am available for travel and for location in other countries.

If you believe that I might be suited for the position, I would be glad to meet with you anytime and to provide whatever further documents you need. Names of references, both at Weymarsh and elsewhere, will be provided on request.

Thanks for your attention to my application. I look forward to hearing from you.

Sincerely,

Rutland Rogers

Enclosure

Practice: Writing Good Letters

ACME GARDEN SUPPLY COMPANY
3333 Broad Street
New Brunswick, New Jersey 08903
1-800-839-0007

    You are a customer service manager for this company. You receive a letter from Mrs. Batt in St. Louis, enclosing a broken lawnmower wheel. She says the wheel was broken when she opened the carton, and she wants a replacement.

    You send the wheel to the Parts Department, which reports back to you that the wheel is at least seven years old, is badly damaged, and has been run over by a blue automobile. A replacement wheel costs $74.95 plus shipping. It is Acme policy not to provide free replacement parts when the company is not at fault.

    Write to Mrs. Batt.

RÉSUMÉS

Altogether too much of a big deal is made about résumés. Those ads that scream **"Can't get a job? Maybe it's your résumé!"** are pigwash. Likewise the new wave of innovative-creative-dynamic-revolutionary résumés-with-a-difference—these are just gimmicks being peddled by professional résumé-writing people, each of whom is trying to build a reputation by outdoing the others in originality, without regard for results. Don't worry about such pickinesses; spend your time doing substantive things.

Nonetheless, you do have to have a résumé, and a bad one can hurt you. In fact, there really isn't such a thing as a good résumé—instead there are only acceptable ones and bad ones. Your concern is to be sure yours isn't bad.

Think about what happens to the résumé once it's received in the company, and you'll understand. A single job advertisement sometimes elicits 5,000 applications. A boss faced with such a pile of résumés will simply say to an assistant, "Go through and pick out the 25 most likely looking." And thus the assistant is sent out on a search-and-destroy mission, looking for a reason, any reason, to throw out 4,975 résumés. Sloppy appearance is a reason; so is overly neat appearance (printed on vellum with five-color ink). Too little detail is a reason; so is too much. Anything that attempts to be cute (pink paper, perfume, sensational headlines) is another. Thus you can't win by having a super-good résumé; all you can hope to do is to avoid having one that irritates the assistant.

Avoiding the trash heap is mostly luck, but following these 10 short suggestions will help:

1. Make it neat and instantly legible.
2. Put it all on one page if you can, or two anyhow. Engineers and lawyers may require three or four.

3. Be factual, not subjectively descriptive. Say "retail clerk," not "enthusiastic self-starter." It's okay for them to advertise for an "enthusiastic self-starter," but it's not okay for you to call yourself one. Let the facts about what you've done show that you are what they're looking for. Repeat: don't tell them; show them.

4. Tell not what you were called but what you actually did: not just "junior executive" but "sold gloves," "supervised 14 switchboard operators," "took inventory," "abstracted articles," "established statistical reference file," and so on.

5. Build up your relevant points, not your irrelevant ones. Include what you want them to know about you. Do not say you are the Eastern Regional Bubble Gum Champion because they probably don't want a person who regards that as a major accomplishment. Do, on the other hand, tell them that you have made a special study of computer applications in small-business accounting practices, even if, to you, that's less important than bubble gum is. Be truthful but selective. And by the way, do by all means use different résumés for different job applications, so that you can present the most pertinent credentials for each one.

6. Build up your strong points, not your weak ones. If you have herpes, keep it to yourself. Simply say "Good health" and they'll probably never even wonder why you didn't say "Excellent health." Tell about the time you spent working for IBM, not about the time you spent in the State Penitentiary.

7. Even though you shouldn't try to attract attention with an unusual format, you can and should mention unusual things you've done: summer with a U.S. senator's office, three years in Uganda, volunteer firefighting, organizing camps for urban kids, and so on. Let the substance, not the style or appearance, be what distinguishes your résumé from the pack.

8. Remember that employers are interested in performance, not status. In describing your "Objective," don't tell them you want "a challenging position commensurate with my talents." Instead, stress that what you really want to do is to build bridges, design financial controls, advise stockholders, sell computer systems, and such things.

9. Be sure the telephone number you give is one that will be answered by somebody. Don't give your home number if you're somewhere else all day.
10. Do not include a photograph.

It's always a bad idea for a book to give examples of résumés, since people then go and copy them slavishly instead of inventing their own. Nonetheless, here are two examples of acceptable ones—the first a strictly chronological one, the second constructed along functional lines. You will notice that they include five types of information: job objective, experience, education, personal information, and references. These are fairly standard categories, but you shouldn't take that statement to mean that all résumés have to have exactly these same five. Some will have fewer (in fact the second one here does), and some will have other categories not included in this list. In short, these are examples, not models.

DEXTER McC. WHITEWASH
42 Long Oak Avenue
Royal Grove, New Jersey 07777
(201-670-9055)

OBJECTIVE: Career in advertising, involving both creative and management responsibilities.

EDUCATION: MBA candidate (part time), Weymarsh Business School; degree expected 2014. Joint emphasis in Finance and Marketing.

BA (Art and Literature), Weymarsh College, 2004. Special studies included two courses in Commercial Art and one in Writing for Business and Industry. Also participated in team internship designing graphics for Widener Communications. Cumulative average: 3.64.

EXPERIENCE: 2004-08 Assistant to the Director of Sales, Michie Magazine Publications. Worked with the Director in planning and overseeing expansion from 40 to 90 outlets nationwide.

2008- Director of Marketing, Textbook Division, Martin Book Company. Supervise a staff of 15. Have overseen successful introduction of 24 textbooks in markets previously dominated by major companies.

PERSONAL: Married, two children.

REFERENCES: Available on request.

Example of a Functional Résumé

Résumé: DAISY RICKMAN
4932 Old Brook Road
Richland, New York 10200
telephone 516-627-7387

Job Objective: Management work in a hospital or extended care facility.

Experience: In nursing—
North Shore Nursing Home, Long Island, 1999-2005.
Promoted from Staff Nurse to Acting Assistant Supervisor
and finally to Assistant Supervisor, night shift.

Long Oaks Rest Home, Newark, NJ, 2000-2005.
Supervisor, night shift.

Silver Stream Extended Care Facility, Valley Cove,
NY, 2006- . Supervisor, day shift.

In management—
Sears, Roebuck (Utica, NY), 1998-2000
(part-time). Assistant to the Manager, retail store.

Education: BS in Nursing, Utica College, 1988. Special work in
long-term and geriatric care.

MBA, Weymarsh Business School, 2011. Special work in
management of not-for-profit institutions, arts management,
and personnel management.

References:

Rosetta Kristin	Parker Schafer
North Shore Nursing Home	Long Oaks Home
Rabsen, NY 10119	Box 136
	Newark, NJ 07104

Joan Stumpf, Director
Silver Stream Extended Care Facility
Valley Cove, NY 11078

INTERVIEW QUESTIONS

When you are going to be interviewed, be absolutely prepared for six questions:

1. **Tell me about yourself. (Alternatively: Walk me through your résumé.)**

   Don't just give a chronological history. Focus on your interests, experiences, abilities, and aspirations.

2. **Why do you want to be a _____?**

   The focus here is on your interest in *this kind of work*.

3. **Why do you think you would be a good _____?**
   (Alternatively: Why should we hire you for this job?)

   Focus on *your qualifications* to do the work—good with statistics, good with people, knowledgeable about polymer chemistry.

4. **Why do you want to work for _____ Company?**

   The focus here is on *this particular company* and how you have been attracted to it. It helps if you've done your homework and have some specific knowledge about it.

5. **Where do you see yourself 5 (or 10) years from now?**

   Have something fairly specific to say. Do you want to keep on doing this kind of work? Do you want to supervise it? Do you want to stay in this location? Talk about the *work* you want to be doing, not about the title or status you want to have.

6. **Do you have any questions?**

   Your answer should be yes. Do your homework in advance, and be ready with some intelligent questions.

TALKS

Since spoken presentations—even simple ones like telling your boss what you've discovered about a certain account or a prospective investment—are far more common than written ones, and at least as disastrous, they deserve a whole manual to themselves. For the present, however, be content with 11 general rules.

Rule 1. Know What You're Talking About

As painful as it is to hear poor speakers, it's still worse to hear polished ones who don't know their subjects. No amount of beautiful oratory, dramatic gestures, and other such baloney can cover up ignorance or unpreparedness. Spend 95 percent of your time on your subject, the other 5 percent on the presentation.

Rule 2. Don't Read and Don't Memorize

You are talking *to* somebody. If you read or recite, then you're behaving just as you would if nobody were there. And the audience will know it right away and react accordingly: people simply don't listen to talks that are read or memorized. You should use notes to remind yourself what points you want to make, but you must not write out your sentences. Just look at the people and talk to them.

Rule 3. Begin by Telling Us WHAT You're Going to Say and WHY We Should Care

"I am opposed to the proposed acquisition of the Schlerg Company for four reasons" is a good opening: it tells that you're opposed and that you're going to say four things to show why. Another good opening is "As I've been analyzing the causes of the failure of this product, I've tried to answer three questions: how it happened, what we can do about it, and how we can prevent such things in the future." And don't underestimate the part about "why we should care." You'll get vastly improved attention if you tell your audience from the very first why the subject is important to them.

Rule 4. Establish a Structure That You Will Follow

Tell your readers something about how many points you're going to make, or how many reasons, or how many examples, or how long, or at least something, as illustrated in those openings in Rule 3. If you simply start off by saying "A bad public image is one reason I oppose the acquisition," then your listeners have no way of knowing whether that's 1 reason out of 2, or 4, or 50—that is, 50 percent, 25 percent, or 2 percent of your argument. It matters, both in how much importance they attach to each reason and in how well they remember afterward what points you made—and also in how awake they stay while you're talking. This is a pretty important concept. Remember that a *reader* can tell, just by looking, how long a written report is; but a *listener* hasn't got any way of knowing whether you're talking for a minute or an hour or a day. You will achieve vastly improved attention and retention if you tell the audience in advance how many points you're making, so they can mentally check them off as you talk.

Rule 5. Tell No Jokes

Make no cute remarks; don't say how glad you are to be there; don't address ladies, gentlemen, distinguished speakers, honored guests, officers, staff members, friends, visitors, inmates. Do not say "In conclusion I would like to say."

Rule 6. Think of Visual Aids as Evidence to Be Commented On

If you use flipcharts, transparencies, PowerPoint, or other visual aids, use them as something you want to show your audience, not as something to be read to them. You might not want to use them at all; sometimes everything is clear enough without them. But when you do use them, at least have the decency not to read them word by word to your audience, as if you were giving the first grade a reading lesson. Also, never use cutesy signs, like a picture of some thumb tacks while you smirkingly say "Let's get down to brass tacks, oh, ha, ha, ha, chuckle, chuckle, chuckle, tee hee hee." Barf.

What you absolutely do need PowerPoint, transparencies, or flipcharts for is graphs, figures, statistics, numbers. It's almost impossible for an audience to take in a numerical discussion without having the numbers in front of them; and even if the point is somehow clear at the moment, it will be forgotten immediately unless there's something to look at.

Rule 7. Know How (and When) to Use the Projector

If you do use either PowerPoint or an overhead projector, be sure you know how before the presentation begins. The one thing you most of all absolutely positively don't want to look like when you're doing a business presentation is a certified Dumb Klutz—and if you can't get the machine running right, *you lose*. Practice with whatever equipment you're going to use. Furthermore, be sure whatever you use has a typeface big enough to be readable from the back of the room. And finally—important point—don't show anything on the screen until you're ready to talk about it. If you turn it on earlier, your audience will be reading the screen instead of listening to what you're saying. Tell people what you're going to be showing them, and then, when they have been fully prepped and are all eager to see it, turn it on and show them.

One more thing: If you use PowerPoint, be sure to remember why you're there and what you're doing. Distracting graphics (like data fluttering in from four sides) are truly irritating. They signal to the audience that you've spent more effort on showing them the clever things you can do than on the point you're trying to make.

Rule 8. Keep It Simple

People are terrible listeners and rememberers; they probably won't remember a tenth of what you say. Make sure the tenth you want them to remember is what stands out in their minds. Don't clutter the talk with any complexities you could have left out. A limited number of points, clearly stated and clearly summarized at the end, is a must.

Rule 9. Anticipate Questions and Objections

Don't get caught by surprise. Think about what questions people are likely to ask, and have an answer prepared—or better still, answer the question before they ask. Things like "How much is this going to cost?" or "Who's going to pay for all this?" or "Has this ever been tried before?" are entirely predictable. If you fumble around while looking for an answer or admit you had never thought of the question, you drastically undercut your credibility. If somebody asks a question you don't know the answer to, you can promise to research it and get back later, or you can divert the question to something you do know about, as in "I don't have any specific figures about steel imports last year, but I do know that overall imports were up 19 percent."

Rule 10. End by Asking for Questions

When you've finished your presentation, simply say "I'll be glad to answer questions if you have any," or "Are there any questions?" That way you send a signal to the audience to let them know that's all you're going to say—and it's considerably less awkward than saying "Thank you" as if you're expecting thunderous applause.

Rule 11. Rehearse

Deliver the talk in an empty room. Deliver it in front of a mirror. Deliver it into an audiorecorder. Deliver it in front of a video camera. Deliver it to somebody, even if just your dog or cat. Do it at least nine times and always out loud, not just silently to yourself. Such rehearsing doesn't mean you will be memorizing; in fact it will be different every time you do it. What the rehearsing will do is to make you considerably more at ease, and it will let you know what parts you are going to have trouble with. As any teacher can tell you, it's easy to fool yourself into thinking you know something well, only to find, when you try to tell it to somebody else, you didn't really know it well enough at all. In rehearsing *out loud*, you'll find out.

Part V

SAMPLE REPORTS

A REALLY BAD REPORT

FICTITIOUS UNIVERSITY
Springfield, Kansas

To: President McGinnis
From: Marlon Smith, Assistant
Date: November 24, 20–
Subject: Dediums Company as an internship partner

The Dediums Company was founded in 1924 and is
incorporated under the laws of the state of Delaware.
It employed 34,862 people as of 2010. It operates in 13
countries. Since 1999 the president has been John Hare.

Irrelevant

Irrelevant, vague
Point unclear
Relevance unclear

*Reader should know
the point by now—
whether yes or no—
as well as the order
the report will follow.*

Location
The company has its main office in Norwalk, Connecticut,
but it has branches all around the country. It also has
overseas operations. According to some sources, it plans
to expand to other locations in the future.

*Subheading must state
the point that's
going to be made.*

*Information here is
vague, and its
relevance is unclear.*

Business

Sales last year amounted to $2.7 million. The number of

topic.

employees has increased 5 percent in the last 10 years.
Approximately 421 people work at the headquarters site.

Subhead must state point, not just

Are these figures good or bad? What's the point?

Officers

The following are the officers of the company:

    John Hare, President

    William McVey, Vice President

    Joseph Markovy, Treasurer

Totally useless

Recommendation

I recommend that we establish an internship program
with this company.

Should have come first, and should tell the reasons for the recommendation

Anybody who wrote a report as bad as this would be, and should be, fired immediately. Besides the fact that it wastes the reader's time by being disorganized and by presenting irrelevant and unclear information, it carries no persuasive power at all because it does not show the reasoning that led to the conclusion.

A BAD REPORT

Fictitious University
Springfield, Kansas

To: President McGinnis
From: Dagmar Smith, Assistant
Date: November 24, 20—
Subject: Dediums Company as an internship partner

You have asked me to research the Dediums
Company to see if it is a good company for Fictitious
University to include in the list of companies we use for our
internship program. After carefully considering the
information, I have concluded that it is a good company.
I will discuss here the financial performance, the
reputation, and the company's future.

Obvious from the
subject line

Tell the points you will
make, not just the order.
By now the reader
should know whether
the answer is yes or no.

Financial Performance
In 2012 the Dediums Company reported earnings
of $923,546 on sales of $2.7 million. Its stock is now selling
at $64 a share. Debt amounts to $3.3 million, of which
$2 million is long term. Acquisition of Eugene Industries
last year increased the value of the company by nearly
20 percent.

Subhead must tell the
point—what about the
performance?
Good facts, but not
organized in support
of any overall point
Numbers are not
compared.

Reputation

The American Retail Association has placed the Dediums Company as number 12 on its list of Reliable Companies. The Association of Immigrant Workers awarded Dediums a rating of "Good Employer." No significant lawsuits appear to be pending against the company.

Should state point

12 out of how many?

Is "good" the highest? "Significant" and "appear" suggest hidden problems.

Future

The company announced last fall that it plans to expand its overseas operations, as well as continue its search for suitable acquisitions at home.

Bad subheading

Details needed

Sources

Google
www.dediums.com
Wall Street Journal

Vague
Not a reliable source
Must specify date and article

This report is extremely weak, even though it appears to make an attempt at organization. By not adopting internal organization principles, it forces the reader to read through the entire report to learn what its findings are, and even then the results are not especially convincing.

A GOOD INTERNAL REPORT

Fictitious University
Springfield, Kansas

To: President McGinnis
From: Sharissa Smith, Assistant
Date: November 24, 20—
Subject: Dediums Company as an internship partner

I recommend that we adopt the Dediums Company as one of our internship partners. The company has a good financial record, is a model corporate citizen, and shows great promise for the future.

Clear statement of the conclusion and the order of presentation

Excellent Financial Condition

Dediums is a very solid company, as evidenced by its continually growing sales and by recent favorable developments in the household products industry. Sales, which were only $925,000 as recently as 2003, have nearly tripled to more than $2.7 million today, growth that is more than twice as fast as that of its nearest competitor in the household products industry. Furthermore, over the past five years a clear trend in consumer preferences away from imports and toward American products has turned the entire industry around. What appeared to be a declining sector just a few years ago now appears to be permanently prosperous, and the company is well positioned to remain strong.

Subheading makes point clear.
Point stated at the start
Order of details established

Detail 1; clear comparisons
Detail 2

Restatement of point

Fine Corporate Citizen

Both locally and nationally, Dediums has distinguished itself as the kind of company Fictitious University would like to be associated with. In every one of its seven locations in the United States, it has made a effort to be engaged in community improvement programs, as attested to by awards it has received in Des Moines, Santa Fe, Portland (Maine), and Wayne (New Jersey), and by extensive press coverage in its other three cities. Its outstanding employee relations policies have brought it national attention, for example on *60 Minutes* and in a series of articles in the *Chicago Sun-Times*. It has also been mentioned favorably in *Working Mother* magazine and in the *AARP Bulletin*. I did not find even a single piece of negative evidence concerning Dediums' social performance.

Promising Future

Finally, all signs point to good years ahead for the company. Expansion from within, acquisitions and mergers, and a growing public image make it inevitable that the company will be around for a long time. Management has made clear, although of course without releasing details, that the product line will continue to be enlarged gradually. Dediums has already acquired several smaller companies and plans to continue doing so. And recent surveys indicate that the name of the company as well as the brand names of its leading product lines have become increasingly familiar to the public over the past 15 years. We can be as confident as it's possible to be that the company will be around for many years to serve as an internship partner.

Subheading states point.
Point clear, order clear

Good details about local

Good details about national

Strong restatement

Subheading makes point clear.
Point made clear from the first.
Three-part division made clear.

Point 1

Point 2

Point 3

Restatement
No summary needed for a simple report like this one

Sources

Brand News (online)

Corporate Social Responsibility News (online)

Encyclopedia of American Industries

Letter to Stockholders, Dediums, December 31, 2011

PR News (online)

Value Line

In an informal report like this one, a mere list of sources is sufficient documentation.

Any reader will be able to read this report at top speed and see not only the overall point but the reasoning that has led to the conclusion. It would be impossible not to understand the point here or not to be persuaded that it is the correct one.

A GOOD EXTERNAL REPORT

The following is also a good report, this one external and somewhat more formal. In this instance, one company has sought an opinion from an outside consultant, and this is the resulting report.

JL Consultants
447 Kildeer Avenue
Peyton Lakes, NJ 07498

Mr. Alden DeRenay, President
Economic Reporting Co., Inc.
392 Comshock Lane
Wilhelm, NY 10908

Dear Mr. DeRenay:

Enclosed is the report you requested, giving our opinion about whether the Arthur Andersen financial firm actually deserved to be driven out of business following the Enron scandal or was instead unjustly forced to take the blame for others' mistakes.

Please let me know if you have questions or need further information.

Yours truly,

Malcolm N. Morland

Enclosure

Arthur Andersen: The Fall Was Justified

The collapse of the Enron Corporation in 2001 sent shocks through the whole economy—not just the energy business but investments, pension funds, employment, tax revenues, and more. One significant consequence of the whole affair was the closing of the venerable Arthur Andersen accounting firm, an event that would have been inconceivable just a year earlier. It seemed so impossible, in fact, that people have argued, and probably still do, that the firm could not have deserved such a fate but instead was a scapegoat for other people's actions. Five main claims prevail: that the firm had a stellar reputation for ethics, that its actions were not wrong, that other firms were doing the same things Andersen was doing, that the Houston office alone was responsible for problems, and that, after all, the U.S. Supreme Court did vindicate the firm by overturning its conviction. Closer examination reveals all five of these claims to be flawed. This report will show that Arthur Andersen unquestionably violated its charter and the public trust by committing several serious misdeeds.

Claim 1. Andersen Was an Outstandingly Ethical Firm

Beyond any question, it is true that the Arthur Andersen accounting firm had indeed been famous for its ethics during almost all of its existence. In the last decade of the twentieth century, however, the company had dropped its ethical stance and allowed the profit motive to dominate.

A story told over and over within the company recounted how founder Andersen himself, in the company's first year (1904), had been asked by a railroad client to certify something that was manifestly untrue. His reply was that "there is not enough money in the city of Chicago" to get him to sign off on the document.[1] The company proudly and relentlessly stuck to this principle of uprightness through most of its nearly century-long existence, acquiring such nicknames as "the conscience of the accounting industry" and "the self-righteous preacher of the profession." In 1964 it severely reprimanded one of its clients, Bethlehem Steel, for improper accounting, and on one occasion it even publicly criticized the accounting policies of the Securities and Exchange Commission. It further

---

[1] Brown, "Arthur Andersen's Fall from Grace," *Wall Street Journal*, June 7, 2002.

added to its reputation as "the most upright of the nation's accounting firms" by funding such projects as a seven-year $5 million cooperative venture with over 500 universities to raise awareness of the importance of ethics in business. The name of the firm was virtually synonymous with ethics.[2]

By the 1990s, however, the emphasis had shifted. The firm's original four "cornerstones" had been service to the firm, quality audits, good management of staff, and profits for the firm, but now the first three slipped in significance and the fourth grew. The firm adopted a policy of requiring partners to retire at age 56, and one result was a change to a younger, more profit-hungry generation of partners less concerned with the ethical tradition. An observer noted problems as far back as 1986, and by the mid-1990s they had grown worse. The pressure to make money overrode all other considerations. Andersen had ceased to be an ethics-dominated company.[3]

Claim 2. Andersen's Actions Were Not Wrong

Andersen claimed that it was being punished as a scapegoat for the sins of others, but the evidence of wrongdoing is very strong. The CEO said his firm did nothing wrong, that Enron had spun out of control, that "economics" was to blame, and that in fact Andersen had repeatedly warned Enron about problems. With the respect to the last of these statements, several examples do exist in which the accounting firm registered some resistance to what Enron was doing—for example, refusing to approve one or another scheme and requiring restatement of earnings—but these incidents occurred quite late, long after most of the problems had surfaced.[4] The great majority of the evidence shows that Andersen was in fact guilty in many

---

[2] Brown, "Andersen's Fall from Grace"; Flynn McRoberts, "The Fall of Andersen," *Chicago Tribune*, Sept. 1, 2002; Bethany McLean, *The Smartest Guys in the Room* (NY: Portfolio, 2003), 143; Tepper School of Business, Carnegie Mellon University, "Arthur Andersen Case Studies in Business Ethics," http://web.tepper.cmu.edu/ethics/aa/arthurandersen.htm.

[3] Brown, "Andersen's Fall from Grace"; McLean, *The Smartest Guys*, pp. 140-141.

[4] McRoberts, "The Fall of Andersen"; "Ties to Enron Blinded Andersen," *Chicago Tribune*, Sept. 3, 2002; McLean, *The Smartest Guys in the Room*, pp. 316-318, 407-408; Salter, *Innovation Corrupted*, pp. 116, 148, 348.

respects, including not just failure to report problems but actually committing errors, compromising its independent status, and destroying evidence. Examples of failure to speak up about manifest errors, which is the principal duty of an auditor, are well documented.[5] In addition, actual malfeasance, such as shifting losses from one entity to another, recording profits long before they were even close to being realized, and approving a devious deal involving a Nigerian barge, also clearly took place.[6]

Next, Andersen's failure to maintain independence from its client is evident in several ways. One was extensive close personal hob-nobbing among top executives from the two firms, and another was the intermingling of workforces to the extent that more than 100 Andersen employees had offices inside the Enron building. Another compromise with strict independence was that Arthur Andersen served as both internal accountant and external auditor for the same firm, with the obvious result that it was then merely auditing its own work. But probably the most blatant of all the compromises was that Andersen's consulting division was devising accounting schemes and then putting pressure on its auditing division to approve them. When an Andersen auditor named Carl Bass refused to approve a certain plan, Enron demanded that he be removed from the project and replaced with somebody who would approve, and Andersen complied. Enron officials later said they didn't realize that Andersen was not operating independently. As dubious as that claim is, the claim that Andersen officials weren't aware of the problem is even more impossible to believe.[7]

And finally, destruction of evidence is probably, more than any other charge, what brought the Andersen firm down. Although it tried to argue that it was merely complying with an established policy that required it to retain only "essential information to support our conclusions," the evidence points strongly in the other direction. In the Waste Management case just a few years earlier, Andersen's

---

[5] McLean, p. 190; Salter, pp. 78, 105-106, 190.

[6] McRoberts, "Ties to Enron Blinded Andersen."

[7] McRoberts, "Ties to Enron Blinded Andersen"; Salter, pp. 207-209; McLean, p. 143; McRoberts, "Civil War Splits Andersen"; Brown, "Arthur Andersen's Fall from Grace"; McRoberts, "Repeat Offender Gets Stiff Justice"; McLean, pp. 295-297; Salter, pp. 356-362.

failure to destroy files had provided the government with damning evidence, and thus the firm was now taking no chances. Andersen employees worked around the clock for several days shredding documents, destroying more in one week than would normally have been destroyed in a whole year. Even after the SEC raised the status of its inquiry to the "formal investigation" level, the shredding continued, in clear violation of the law. Massive numbers of e-mails were also deleted. When the company later tried to place the blame on David Duncan, its partner who had supervised the destruction, he joined forces with the government and testified against his former employer, putting the final seal on its doom. After that, it was impossible for Arthur Andersen to argue that it had done nothing wrong.[8]

Claim 3. Other Firms Were Doing the Same Thing Andersen Did

An Arthur Andersen spokesman issued a statement saying that "the issues and concerns raised affect the entire profession and not only Andersen." Technically, he was correct. Deloitte & Touche had had an embarrassing scandal with regard to Adelphia, for example, and KPMG with Xerox. Undoubtedly also, Vinson & Elkins, the law firm that advised Enron, should have shared in the blame for the company's fraud and bankruptcy, as should various government oversight bodies and some politicians. But Andersen's problems were far more numerous than just those at Enron. As far back as the 1980s the firm had incurred censure for not reporting problems at carmaker DeLorean, and subsequently problems were encountered with its work for Waste Management, Global Crossing, Qwest, Colonial Realty, and finally WorldCom. Moreover, the sheer extent of Andersen's intimate involvement with the whole Enron affair was unparalleled. The guilt of others does not mitigate its transgressions.[9]

---

[8] McRoberts, "Civil War Splits Andersen," *Chicago Tribune*, Sept. 2, 2002; McLean, p. 381; McRoberts, "Ties to Enron Blinded Andersen"; Fox, pp. 271-272; McRoberts, "Repeat Offender Gets Stiff Justice," *Chicago Tribune*, Sept. 4, 2002.

[9] Brown, "Arthur Andersen's Fall from Grace"; McRoberts, "Civil War Splits Andersen"; McRoberts, "Repeat Offender Gets Stiff Justice"; Peter Lattman, "The Vinson & Elkins-Enron Connection: The Plot Thickens," *Wall Street Journal*, June 1, 2006; Committee Staff Investigation of the Federal Energy Regulatory Commission's Oversight of Enron Corp: Staff Memorandum. United States Congress, Senate, Committee on Governmental Affairs, 2004; McRoberts, "Ties to Enron Blinded Andersen."

Claim 4. The Houston Office Alone, Not the Whole Firm, Was Guilty

One of the weakest contentions by Arthur Andersen is that the national firm itself did not know about and would never have approved the actions that its Houston office was taking. Top executives claimed that decisions were made in the field by engagement partners, not by the central office, and that the federal government should have focused on the local branch and left the rest of the firm alone. But although it might be true that the Houston partners had acted on their own, the fact that they were permitted to do so, following a policy of decentralization that the firm had adopted in 1989, was a strong indictment. "This is precisely why this firm should be indicted," a member of the government's prosecutorial team said. Since each branch was being encouraged to build up the greatest profits possible, and the central headquarters was doing nothing to exert control, the entire firm deserved to be held accountable.[10]

Claim 5. The Supreme Court Overturned Andersen's Conviction

Finally, the fact that the U.S. Supreme Court reversed a lower court decision that had found Arthur Andersen guilty of destroying evidence cannot be taken as a defense for what the firm did. In the lower court, the judge had instructed the jury that Andersen could be found guilty even if its employees hadn't been aware that what they were doing was wrong. The Supreme Court ruled only that the judge had erred in giving such instructions, and thus it set aside the verdict on those narrow grounds. Nothing in the ruling said anything about whether or not the file shredding and e-mail deletions amounted to obstruction of justice. The decision did not declare Arthur Andersen innocent; it merely said that a judge had made a procedural error.[11]

In short, all the arguments made in defense of Arthur Andersen fail to stand up under scrutiny. Close examination shows that the once-venerable firm was no longer venerable. It had committed many transgressions, and in our professional opinion it deserved to be closed down.

---

[10] Richard M. Steinberg, "Corporate Culture: Who Failed, Who Got It Right," *Compliance Week*, Feb. 18, 2009; Brown, "Arthur Andersen's Fall from Grace"; McRoberts, "Repeat Offender Gets Stiff Justice."

[11] Mary Flood, "Andersen Document Shredding Conviction Overturned," *Houston Chronicle*, June 1, 2005.

List of Works Cited

Brown, Ken, and Ianthe J. Dugan. "Arthur Andersen's Fall from Grace Is a Sad Tale of Greed and Miscues," *Wall Street Journal*, June 7, 2002.

Flood, Mary. "Andersen Document Shredding Conviction Overturned," *Houston Chronicle*, June 1, 2005.

Lattman, Peter. "The Vinson & Elkins-Enron Connection: The Plot Thickens," *Wall Street Journal*, June 1, 2006.

McLean, Bethany. *The Smartest Guys in the Room*. New York: Portfolio, 2003.

McRoberts, Flynn. "The Fall of Andersen," *Chicago Tribune*, Sept. 1, 2002

_____."Civil War Splits Andersen," *Chicago Tribune*, Sept. 2, 2002.

_____. "Ties to Enron Blinded Andersen," *Chicago Tribune*, Sept. 3, 2002.

_____."Repeat Offender Gets Stiff Justice," *Chicago Tribune*, Sept. 4, 2002.

Salter, Malcolm S. *Innovation Corrupted: The Origins and Legacy of Enron's Collapse*. Cambridge: Harvard University Press, 2008.

Steinberg, Richard M. "Corporate Culture: Who Failed, Who Got It Right," *Compliance Week*, Feb. 18, 2009.

Tepper School of Business, Carnegie Mellon University. "Arthur Andersen Case Studies in Business Ethics" (http://web.tepper.cmu.edu/ethics/aa/arthur andersen.htm).

United States Congress, Senate, Committee on Governmental Affairs. Committee Staff Investigation of the Federal Energy Regulatory Commission's Oversight of Enron Corp: Staff Memorandum. 2004.

Part VI

THE APPEARANCE OF THE FINISHED DOCUMENT

Pages 23 to 25 explained why the appearance of your paper is important. The following items provide more details to assure that decency standards are met. Above all, just let good sense guide you: attractiveness and instant legibility are what count.

Paper
- White.
- 8½ by 11 inches (21.59 by 27.94 centimeters).
- Heavy enough to keep the next page from showing through.
- Never use onion-skin paper, except in private.

Typing
- Black cartridge of recent vintage. It's not enough for the cartridge itself to look black; the print that comes out of it must look black too. If it's turning gray, get a new one. There's no such thing as a permanent cartridge; they have to be replaced every now and then.
- Double-space all reports; single-space all letters.
- Big fat margins on left and right sides and at the top and bottom—at least 1¼ inches (3.175 centimeters) on each of the four edges.
- One side of the paper only—absolutely—always, whether you handwrite or type.

Punctuation
- Commas and periods always go inside the quotation marks, regardless of where they logically should belong, like "this," or "that." Other punctuation marks go where they logically ought to go.
- Two spaces after a period or a colon; one space after a comma or a semicolon.
- A dash consists of two hyphens, with no spaces around them--like that.

- A hyphen consists of one hyphen, with no spaces around it, that-like.
- Only one period at the end of a sentence, even if you have an abbreviation, like this: "He works at Time Warner, Inc."
- Always leave *two spaces* after a period at the end of a sentence. The extra space is a signal to the reader that it's the end, not just an abbreviation or a decimal point.

Page Numbers
- Yes, number all pages after the first one. Be consistent about where you put the numbers.

Format and Layout
- If it's an internal communication, that is, one person to another within the same company, simply use the memorandum format, like this:

To: Mr. Daniel
From: Egbert Egbert

Subject: Labor unrest at the Durst plant

Date: November 5, 20—

My research into the unrest at our Durst plant indicates that the problems should be fairly easy to solve. If we can correct some salary inequities, improve safety conditions, and retire one intransigent manager, we should be able to resume full production almost immediately.

1. Salary Inequities Can Be Quickly Corrected
. . . . .

- If, on the other hand, it's an external communication—that is, from somebody outside the company to somebody inside the company (or vice versa)—then of course the memorandum form won't do. An external report should have the title at the top of page 1, and it should be accompanied by a letter of transmittal, something like the following:

Egbert Consulting Company
Newark, NJ

November 5, 20—

Mr. Henry Kent, Pres.
Kent Enterprises, Inc.
1234 West 56 Street
New York, NY 10028

Dear Mr. Kent:

Enclosed is our report on your inventory management system.
If you have further questions after reading the report, please give us a call.

Yours truly,

E. J. Egbert
President

Enclosure

STREAMLINING THE INVENTORY
SYSTEM AT KENT ENTERPRISES

Problems of delivery, tracking, and storage in the Kent Enterprises inventory system have created financial losses of as much as 20 percent in the past five years. To remedy these problems, Egbert Consultants suggests undertaking immediate steps regarding supplier relations, computerized records, and physical facilities.

Establish Close Relationships with Suppliers

. . . . .

Cover Sheet
- If the report is an especially formal one—big, or expensive, or important—then you ought to give it a separate cover page in addition to the letter of transmittal. Keep it simple: title, author, date. But if the report is just a more or less routine one, don't use a separate cover sheet at all.

Fastening
- Some people like a plastic cover because it looks slick and cool; others can't stand it because it tortures the reader by eating up most of the inside margin and constantly flopping shut. Ask what to do. If you get no specific instructions, then just put one staple in the upper left corner. **Never** staple the entire left side.

Date
- Always put the date on whatever you write— memos, reports, letters, notes, everything. Don't omit the date.

Right Margin

- Some people think that justifying the right margin makes a report look better. They're wrong. It simply distracts a reader by creating unnecessary spaces between words. (See?) Don't justify the right margin.

Proofreading

- You must. It's your job, not your reader's.

Appendix

Checklists

The following pages set forth a few checklists that you might use when you've finished writing a report—a sort of self-help guide to figuring out how good a job you've done. Please use these lists intelligently, not robotically. Specifically, observe these cautions:

- Nothing here is absolute; anything can be overdone.
- Nothing here is "correct" if your boss told you to do it some other way.
- Not all these "rules" apply to all reports; it's entirely possible that some situations may have quite different requirements.
- You can follow all these rules and still write a very bad report.

These are, in short, designed not to handcuff you but to help you write a reader-friendly report.

Checklist 1. Format and Appearance of the Report

1. The Format

☐ If an internal report, then headed to-from-subject-date?

☐ If an external report, then headed with a title at the top of page 1 and accompanied by a letter of transmittal?

2. The Paper

☐ 8½ by 11 inches?

☐ White?

☐ Opaque?

3. The Word Processor, Computer, and Printer

☐ Dark print on the page?

☐ Clean-looking?

☐ Pleasant, uncrowded typeface—normally 12-point font?

4. The Appearance of the Report

☐ Double spaced?

☐ Extra space between paragraphs?

☐ Huge margins (1¼ inches or more) on all four sides?

☐ Pages numbered in a conspicuous and consistent place?

5. The Fastening

☐ Pages in the correct order?

☐ Staple in the upper left corner?

Checklist 2. Thesis and the Thesis Paragraph

1. The Thesis

□ Have you decided exactly what your point is—that is, exactly what you want your reader to come away from your report remembering? Can you state it in one sentence?

2. The Thesis Paragraph

□ Does the first paragraph clearly state both *what* and *what order* so that your reader can instantly tell, for certain, exactly what your point is and what will come next?

□ Can your reader tell from this paragraph exactly what the subheadings of the report are going to say?

Checklist 3. Subheadings

1. Their Relation to the Thesis

- [ ] Are the subheadings thesis-like—that is, does each make a point rather than just state a topic?

- [ ] Do these points, as a group, constitute a body of evidence that supports your thesis?

- [ ] Are all subheadings prepared for—that is, announced in advance—in the thesis paragraph? (*Another way to say it:* They must be predictable.)

- [ ] Do these points constitute equal subdivisions of your thesis?

2. The Subheadings Themselves

- [ ] Are they parallel with one another in form—all sentences or all phrases?

- [ ] Are they highlighted in some way—underlined, capitalized, in a different typestyle, and so on—so that they clearly stand out?

Checklist 4. Segment and Paragraph Structure

1. The Segments

☐ Are they clearly demarcated, so that the reader can instantly tell where one stops and the next starts?

☐ Are the headings sufficiently thesis-like that the reader can tell what the point of the whole segment will be?

☐ Does the first sentence of each segment clearly relate to the point of the segment?

2. The Paragraphs

☐ Does the first sentence of each paragraph "say it" so clearly that a reader could get a clear idea of the whole argument simply by reading only the first sentences?

☐ Does the second element in each paragraph "explain it" in such a way that it makes the organization of the rest of the paragraph clear?

☐ Does the rest of the paragraph go on to illustrate each of the points in the promised sequence?

Checklist 5. Sentences and Diction

☐ Are at least 50 percent of your verbs something other than *be* verbs (specifically *am, are, is, was, were, have been, has been, will be*)?

☐ Have you avoided *-tion* words wherever possible?

☐ Have you eliminated all, or nearly all, *there is* and *there are* phrases?

☐ Have you distinguished between major and minor ideas in a sentence by subordinating the minor ones?

☐ Have you combed your sentences for superfluous material, so that what remains aims directly at the point?

☐ Have you used *would* only in an *if* situation and made sure that you have used *possibly, perhaps, maybe, somewhat,* and other such qualifiers only in situations where you really mean to qualify your statements?

☐ Does every *this* and *which* have a clear referent?

☐ Have you steered clear of clichés and "automatic" phrases?

☐ Have you used identical forms—for example, all *-ing*, or all *-ed*, or all *which* phrases—for items in parallel positions in a list?

☐ Have you used the Germanic rather than the Latinate/French word—or at least a simple word rather than a pretentious one—in every situation where you had a choice?

☐ Have you been as specific as possible, replacing general and vague words with particular and specific ones?

☐ Have you avoided monotonous droning by varying the length and pattern of your sentences?

☐ Have you had someone read the report aloud to you?

Checklist 6. Graphs and Charts

☐ Have you illustrated with graphs every statistical statement you make, like sales increases and decreases, projected population growth, comparative labor costs in different countries, and market share?

☐ Have you placed the discussion of each point first, and the graph afterward?

☐ Does each graph make an instantly clear visual point—rising, falling, converging, dominating, and so on?

☐ Does each graph have a thesis-like title, stating the point that the picture shows?

☐ Are all the lines, bars, and axes clearly labeled, including the units of measure?

☐ Did you proofread your graphs, word by word, to catch typographical errors?

Checklist 7. Research

☐ Have you actually defined your topic—the specific question, within the area, that you're trying to come up with an answer to? Are you sure it's not just an "area"?

☐ Have you devised a tentative source-list that includes not only many possible sources, but also a variety (including books, newspapers, magazines, and journals, as well as the Internet)? Are the sources impartial and reliable?

☐ Have you perused each of these tentative sources carefully enough to feel confident that you can make an intelligent decision about whether or not to use it in your research?

☐ Have you actually read each of the items in your working source list, rather than just photocopying them or printing them out? And have you actually taken notes on them, so that you have a clear written record, in your own words, of what the source's point is? And have you kept careful records of things like the page numbers where you found the information?

☐ Are you sure that the thesis (a.k.a. point, conclusion) you've come up with is what the notes add up to?

☐ In devising your final plan, have you been careful to present relevant evidence that clearly supports each point, and have you been careful also not to present more pieces of evidence than necessary?

☐ In the writing, have you followed the rules in Checklists 2, 3, 4, and 5?

Index

About the Author

Carter Daniel began his career as a professor of English literature but switched in mid-stream to teaching Business Communication. He has been Director of Business Communication Programs at the Rutgers Business School, Newark and New Brunswick, since 1978. Before coming to Rutgers, he taught at Kent State University (Ohio) and Upsala College (New Jersey). Internationally, he has taught also at Kuwait University (several times), the University of Tripoli (Libya), the Bahrain Institute of Banking and Finance (as a Fulbright Lecturer), and the Helsinki School of Economics.

Among his publications is *MBA: The First Century* (Bucknell University Press, 1998), a detailed history of graduate business education on the occasion of its centennial. Tracing the development of business schools—their purpose, their curriculum, their reputation—through each decade, it shows marked changes in emphasis from industry-specific to generic, from practical to theoretical, from provincial to global, and from mechanistic to humanistic. One reviewer said "To have done this much research is remarkable. To have woven it together into a coherent narrative is something close to a miracle."

He holds an A.B. from Davidson College, an A.M. from Duke University, a Ph.D. from the University of Virginia, and an M.B.A. from Rutgers University. He and his wife Anita, a librarian, have three grown children.

Readers with questions can write him at cdaniel@andromeda.rutgers.edu.